SCHOOL OF HEALING AND IMPARTATION

SPIRITUAL AND MEDICAL PERSPECTIVES

WORKBOOK

COMPILED BY

RANDY CLARK

"The Kingdom of God is not in word [logos], but in power [dunamis]." - *1 Corinthians 4:20*

Table of Contents

Introduction

1 Corinthians 4:20
"For the kingdom of God is not in word [logos] **but in power** [dunamis]**."** (NKJV)

Today a wide gap exists between theology (what we read in the Bible) and what so many believers actually experience. Many believers are trapped in a "vicious downward spiral." Every time expectation based on theology is not met, disappointment sets in, and the level of expectation for the unseen abates slowly and imperceptibly until it reaches a point where most of the real expectation for the supernatural is lost. As a result, it causes a believer to lose faith and live far below the authority and power that God has promised.

The purpose of our Healing School series is to model, impart, and empower believers by equipping them to reproduce the supernatural work of the Holy Spirit in the area of healing. In Healing School 3, after reviewing some key foundations from Healing School 1, we will cover several advanced topics to equip us for even greater effectiveness in the ministry of Healing, including an understanding of the relationship between faith and medicine.

Over the next four days we are excited about you actively receiving three things:
1. **Revelation** – Allowing your mind and heart to be renewed in the Word of God.
2. **Impartation** – Receiving the anointing and presence of the Holy Spirit for empowerment.
3. **Activation** – Stepping out in faith during the practicum sessions to DO what you have been learning and are being empowered for.

The Healing School lesson notes in this workbook∗ are divided into several sections:
1. ***Lesson Goals*** – A bullet list of what we desire to accomplish in that lesson.
2. ***Introduction*** – This section contains a brief introduction to the lesson topic.
3. ***Key Insights*** – This section contains the main body of notes for the lesson topic.
4. ***Activation/Impartation*** – Some Healing School lessons will include times of **impartation** and/or **activation**! We will give you a "heads up" so you can come prepared to jump in when it's time to swim! **BE READY DURING EVENING SESSIONS IN CASE YOU ARE CALLED UPON TO SHARE WORDS OF KNOWLEDGE OR TO PARTICIPATE IN PRAYER MINISTRY USING THE FIVE-STEP MODEL!**
5. ***Personal Reflection*** – We have found in sessions such as you are about to experience, that SO MUCH can happen with God over the course of just a few days! This notes section is provided for you to conveniently journal your thoughts, ponderings, and experiences as you learn, receive, and walk into what the Holy Spirit has for your life and destiny in Him!

This workbook is a course guide, not a replacement for the Ministry Training Manual. For more comprehensive training we encourage you to utilize this and other Global Awakening resources available from our ministry, along with others' materials made available at the book table.

If you obtained this workbook apart from the Healing School, to get the most out of it, we suggest you attend a Healing School.

Chapter 1: The History of Healing within Christianity

Lesson Goals

1) To understand that God has continued to bless the Church with healing and deliverance in every century.
2) To understand that though God used the Apostles in an unusual manner, He also used deacons, evangelists, and other unnamed Christians who were not in a 5 fold office – Apostles, Prophets, Evangelists, Pastors and Teachers – they were just Christians – little ole me's.
3) To understand the causes for the decrease in healing from the 4th to the 19th Centuries.
4) To understand what God did to reestablish the ministry within the Church.
5) To have a better appreciation of the wonderful place in Church history that we live in today and to have a greater hunger and expectation for the supernatural power of God's presence in your lives.

Introduction

Most Protestants have little, if any, understanding of church history, of what God has done in the past, or how doctrines developed within the history of the Church. This is especially true of the doctrine of Cessationism in regard to healing. It is also true of the beliefs of Dispensationalism, and whole segments of the church which adhere to an "unbelieving" interpretation of miracles, signs and wonders. These viewpoints and others will be considered, including how they affected the ministry of healing within the Church in very negative ways.

Key Insights

I) There is a continuous ministry of healing throughout the Church's history.

A) There has never been a time when healings were not occurring somewhere within the Church.

II) The greatest periods of healing have occurred In the first 300 years of the Church and the last 100 years of the Church.

A) The last 100 years have eclipsed the first 300 years mainly due to large numbers of Christians involved in the ministry of healing.

B) In the last 10 years there has been an outbreak of greater kinds of healings or at least a noticeable increase of them (here I am referring to raising the dead).

III) Considering the factors that led to a demise of healing through the Church.

A) Sociological Factors

1) Constantine conversion and the Edict of Milan, (313 A.D.) Persecution had kept Christianity pure with few hypocrites and nominal Christians.

2) Christianity becoming the official religion of the Roman Empire. (380 A.D.) The Church became flooded with nominal members, and was worse off, as many weren't truly converted to Christ.

3) The fall of the Roman Empire (476 A.D.) and the terrible living conditions of the Dark Ages caused the people to focus on the next life rather than healing for this life. (Fall was 476 A.D.) (Dark Ages - 400-1400 A.D.)

4) Scientific Rationalism – denies miracles and healings (Late 17th - 18th centuries)

5) The soul of the human is rejected and we become the result of chemical impulses in our bodies. Human-kind is dehumanized by the humanist movement.

    a) Result: Modern medicine treats patient's symptoms with medicines more than treating the underlying causes of sickness because the unity of body, soul, and spirit is denied.

    b) This begins to change with the field of psychosomatic medicine which is rediscovering and affirming, though often unaware of the Biblical view of a person as a whole and if one part becomes ill it can affect the other two.

    c) It also is discovering the spiritual aspects of disease, i.e. the soul is the seat of will and emotions.

    d) When the principles of Scripture are not followed the soul becomes sick. I.e.: unforgiveness, bitterness, cynical, judgmental.

B) Theological or Hermeneutical Factors

1) Roman Catholic

    a) Augustine's moving from Warfare World View to Blueprint World View – early 300's

    b) Jerome's mistranslation of James 5:14-15

    c) Thomas Aquinas' synthesis of Christian Theology and Aristotelian Philosophy in *Summa Theologica*- Yet at the end of his life Aquinas had changed. St. Thomas Aquinas, Dec. 6th 1273: ***"I can write no more. All I have written seems so much straw compared with what I have seen and what has been revealed to me."*** Three months later he died on a mission trip for the Pope. Others had to finish his famous *Summa Theologica* and we never knew how his experience would have changed his theology had he lived long enough to process the experience into his theology.

    d) Changing anointing for healing to "Extreme Unction." (*8th – 10th Century, various estimates on the date.*)

    e) Removing supernatural dimension of the "gifts of the Spirit" to natural dimension – see Gregory the Great's (Papacy 590 - 604) list of spiritual gifts.

> The Gifts of the Holy Spirit are now viewed as:
> 1. Wisdom
> 2. Science
> 3. Understanding
> 4. Counsel
> 5. Fortitude
> 6. Piety
> 7. Fear

> *Pope Gregory X: "No longer can the Church say, "Silver and Gold, have I none.""*
> *Thomas Aquinas: "Yes, but neither can it any longer say, "Rise and Walk.""*

    f) Utilizing healings, miracles, dead raisings as evidence of true doctrine or deity of Christ instead of the demonstration of the gospel and the goodness of God as the primary purpose, and evidential as secondary purpose.

g) Not distinguishing the context of Paul's and Jesus' references to suffering. Mistakenly seeing suffering in sickness as carrying our cross and glorifying Jesus in our suffering, instead of persecution and suffering for the gospel.

2) *Protestant*

a) **Cessationism** – to deal with evidentialism of Roman Catholicism on the one hand and on the other hand the subjective prophetic authority of the Anabaptist on the radical side of the Reformation– Authority to be found in the Scriptures alone - Calvin and Luther and other major reformers. Ironically Luther prayed for Melancthon's healing when he was near death and he was healed. Luther also had a gift of faith that resulted in a friend and colleague being healed. In 1540, Lutheran reformer Friedrich Myconius (1490-1546) was sick and about to die. He was so weak he could not speak, but he wrote a farewell letter to his good friend Martin Luther (1483-1546) . . . Luther sent back this response. "I command you in the name of God to The Lord will never let me hear that you are dead, but will permit you to survive me. For this I am praying, this is my will, and may my will be done, because I seek only to glorify the name of God." Myconius lived and outlived Luther by two months.

b) **Dispensationalism** – 1830 John Darby – Plymouth Brethren – not only cessationist, but also had view of end-time church being very weak. This view is ultra pessimistic and has no place for an end-time victorious church or an end-time revival. Ironically, this understanding was based upon a "revelation" Margaret MacDonald received in 1830 in a very esoteric experience. This view was never heard of before 1830. Darby notes thereby popularized in the United States in the Scofield Bible.

c) **Neo-orthodoxy** of Barth and Brunner. Like the reformed tradition Barth was cessationist.

d) **Liberalism** – demythologizing of Rudolph Bultmann, and Paul Tillich.

e) **Fundamentalism** and B.B. Warfield's *Counterfeit Miracles*

f) **Negative view of medicine** by leaders of the Faith Cure Movement of last quarter century of 19th century. This led to people and missionaries dying needlessly. Many positive attributes with this movement, but this was a negative position that hurt the healing movement.

3) *Heresies*

a) **Gnosticism** devalues the flesh and has no place for healing of the body. The human body was evil. God is only concerned with the soul, the good part of the human. (Was already a threat while the last books of the New Testament were being written ca. 90-95 A.D. also major threat to Christianity which Irenaeus fought 125-200, wrote *Against Heresies 175-185*. This was his major work against Gnosticism.

b) **Montanism's abuses** of Prophecies regarding the end-times and asceticism. Began prophesying 165-177 A.D.

c) **Apocalyptic-prophetic time setting** in Montanism and in other groups – this usually happens in renewal or revival movements. I think as heaven comes near, closer, the natural tendency is to read into this experience the fervent expectation of the second coming (Parousia) of Jesus. However, because these views are rejected as heretical the renewal, revival, or rediscovery of the gifts are deemed heretical as well, unfairly. However, this is because of the evidential understanding of the purpose of the gifts. Both Roman Catholics and Protestants have been guilty of this.

d) **Mother Baker Eddy** – Christian Science, which is neither Christian nor Science. In 1875 she published her book "Science and Health"

e) **Latter-Rain Revival** (1947)– manifest sons of God, saints won't die.

f) **Key leaders going into heresy** in latter part of their lives; Alexander Dowie (1847 - 1907) and William Branham (1909 - 1965) both thought they were the Prophet Elijah.

g) **Liberalism** – I believe liberalism is a heresy which denies the historic understanding of the theology of the Church by its denial of the supernatural aspects of Christianity, and the Kingdom of God.

C) Church factors

1) Roman Catholic

a) Middle Age period of moral corruption and failure to correct it.

b) Relegating healings and miracles to the "saints" and accusing common people who moved in power to be involved in witchcraft.

c) Accommodating the charismatic pastors and people by allowing charismatic small groups and fellowships within the Roman Catholic Church and the local church, but not allowing the worship services or the liturgies to be charismatic in expression. - Roman Catholic Penecostal Outpouring (1967, USA)

d) 21st Century scandal of pedophile priests not corrected brings distrust among people

2) Protestant

a) Restricting the ministry of Johann Blumhardt (1805 - 1880) in Germany, a Reformed pastor with a powerful healing ministry at Bad Boll, Germany.

b) Excommunicating London Presbyterian pastor Edward Irving (1792 - 1834) in 1830.

c) Violent rejection of the Pentecostal Movement - 1901-1906, Topeka, KS to Azuza St. Los Angeles, CA

d) Bible Colleges and Seminaries discriminating against Pentecostals and Charismatics, not allowed to attend if one spoke in tongues. i.e. Asbury Theological Seminary.

e) Protestant Mission Board firing missionaries who speak in tongues or teach that healing gifts are available for ministry today. Southern Baptist Mission Board adopted this position in 2007.

f) Denominations disfellowshipping churches if they begin to have charismatic experiences such as: speaking in tongues, falling under the power, healing ministries, prophecies.

g) Accommodating the charismatic pastors and people by allowing charismatic small groups and fellowships within the denomination and the local church, but not allowing the worship services or the liturgies to be charismatic in expression.

h) Moral failures of high visibility leaders: Swaggart, Baker, others.

D) Considering the factors that led to the rediscovery of the Healing ministry for the Church.

1) Roman Catholic

a) Roman Catholic Church never totally embraced Cessationism.

b) Healing happened through the Desert Fathers ca. 300 A.D.

c) Healing happened through some of the newly founded Orders, especially those with more missionary focus.

d) Pope Leo XIII at the end of the 19th century calls for a Novena to the Holy Spirit.

e) Pope John XXIII (1942 - 1965) at the Vatican II prays with emphasis upon the Church experiencing a new Pentecost. Vatican II was closed by Pope Paul 6th in 1965.

2) Protestant

a) Commentary author, Vincent Synan, explaining the French Revolution in 1789 as the fulfillment of the 1,260 days of the book of Revelation with the installation of a prostitute as the goddess of Reason in the Notre Dame church in France, and the Pope sent into exile from Rome. Many Protestants believed we were in the last days and expected a great outpouring of the Holy Spirit and restoration of the gifts.[1]

b) Prophecies made by men like Spurgeon (1834-1892) increased this expectation. His 1857 prophecy came two years before the 1859 Revival in Ireland and one year before the great 1858 Prayer Revival in America. Spurgeon said:

"Another great work of the Holy Spirit, which is not accomplished is the *bringing on of the latter-day glory*. [Italics Synan's] In a few more years—I know not when, I know not how—the Holy Spirit will be poured out in far different style from the present. There are diversities of operations; and during the last few years it has been the case that the diversified operations have consisted of very little pouring out of the Spirit. Ministers have gone on in dull routine, continually preaching—preaching—preaching, and little good has been done. I do hope that a fresh era has dawned upon us, and that there is a better pouring out of the Spirit even now. For the hour is coming, and it may be even now, when the Holy Ghost will be poured out again in such a wonderful manner, that many will run to and fro and knowledge shall be increased—the knowledge of the Lord shall cover the earth as the waters cover the surface of the great deep; when His Kingdom shall come, and His will shall be done on earth as it is in heaven . . . .My eyes flash with the thought that very likely I shall live to see the out-pouring of the Spirit; when "the sons and the daughters of God shall prophesy, and the young men shall see visions, and the old men shall dream dreams."[2]

c) Germany, Switzerland, and England

*   Johann Blumhardt (1805-1880) – German Reformed pastor
*   Dorthea Trudell (Ministry began in 1851)–Switzerland - 10,000 healed through her ministry - started hospitals.
*   George Mueller (1805-1895) - living by faith, trusting God to supply your needs.

d) America

*   Dr. Cullis (1833-1892), Homeopathic Doctor with Hospice-type ministry. Pioneer in healing ministry.
*   Carrie Judd Montgomery (1848-1946)
*   D.L. Moody's (1837-1899) Northfield Conferences in Massachusetts

*   Faith Cure Movement
    *   A.J. Gordon (1836-1895) – Baptist, Boston leading proponent of healing ministry.
    *   A.B. Simpson (1843-1919) – Presbyterian, CMA Founder
    *   Andrew Murray (1828-1917) – Dutch Reformed pastor, devotional author

*   The Pentecostal Movement – emphasis upon the belief that God was restoring all the gifts to the Church. (1901-1906 key dates for beginning of the movement.
    *   Alexander Dowie (1847-1907) - began well but ended poorly
    *   Maria Woodworth-Etter (1844-1924) - Methodist - Holiness - Pentecostal
    *   Dr. Charles Price (1887-1947) – Baptist - Pentecostal
    *   F. F. Bosworth (1877-1958) – not a Pentecostal
    *   E.W. Kenyon (1867-1948) (major influence in his life was A.J. Gordon, not influenced by New Thought as supposed and reported.)
    *   Birth of Pentecostalism – Parham (1873-1929) Jan.1901
    *   Azusa St. Revival (began 1906) - W. J. Seymore (1870-1922) (not so much tongues as the restoration of the gifts of the Spirit for power evangelism is what I believe has contributed to the phenomenal growth within the Pentecostal/Charismatic movements.)
    *   Aimee Simple-McPherson (1890-1944)
    *   John G. Lake (1870-1935) - 100,000 healings in Spokane, WA - Trained healing technicians
    *   Smith Wigglesworth (1859-1947)
    *   1947 Latter Rain Revival
    *   1948 Healing Revival
        *   William Branham (1909-1965) - Key - Angelic Visitations - Began well but ended poorly
        *   Oral Roberts (1915-present)
        *   Jack Coe (1918-1956)
        *   T.L. Osborne (1923-present)
        *   many others
    *   1954 Tommy Hicks – Argentina
    *   1960's Charismatic Renewal
    *   1968-1972 Jesus Movement
    *   1982-1996 John Wimber (1934-1997) -- Vineyard, 3rd wave
    *   1994 Toronto Blessing
    *   Mission work of Rolland and Heidi Baker
    *   Leif Hetland (1966 –present)
    *   Steve Stewart (1952-present)

- Randy Clark (1952-present)
  missions, renewal meetings, Schools of Healing and Impartation and School of Missions, Church Planting, and Supernatural Ministry
- Che Ahn (1956-present)
- Bill Johnson (1951-present)
  Schools of Supernatural Ministry
- Todd Bentley – especially the Lakeland Florida Healing Outpouring

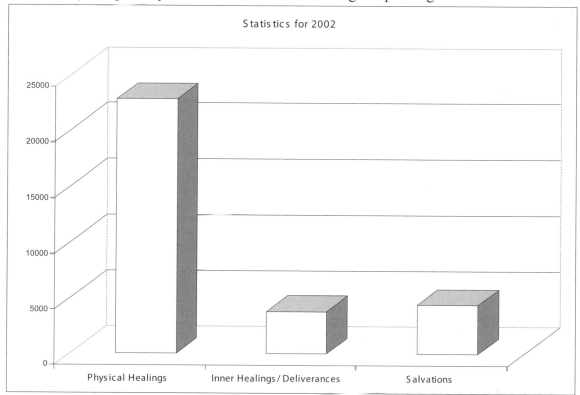

Statistics for 2002

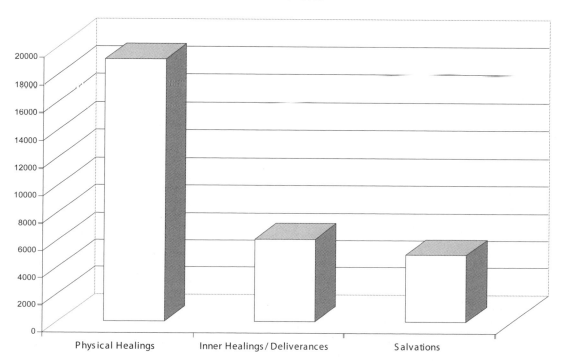

Statistics for 2003

Statistics for 2004 A

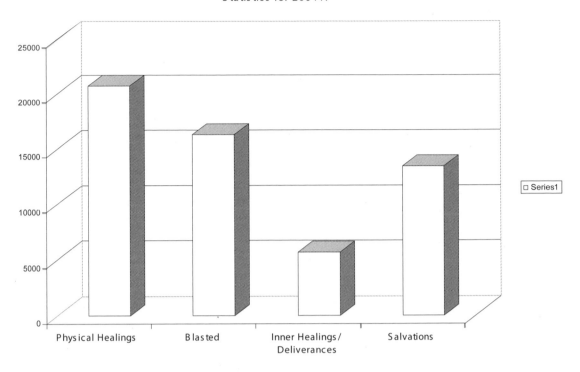

Statistics for 2004 B
(20,781 Physical Healings)

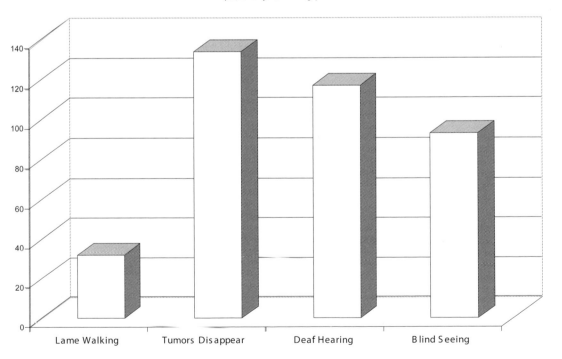

Statistics for 2005 A
(Total Attendance for 2005 was 544,471)
Note: 2005 was first year to India

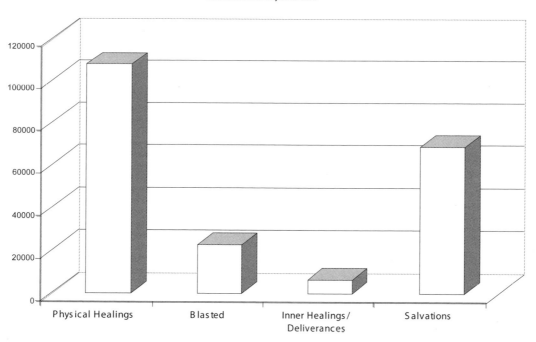

Statistics for 2005 B
(107,910 Physical Healings)

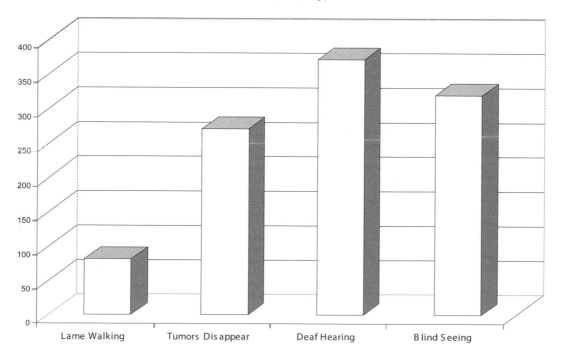

Statistics for 2006 A
(Total Attendance for 2006 was 142,331)

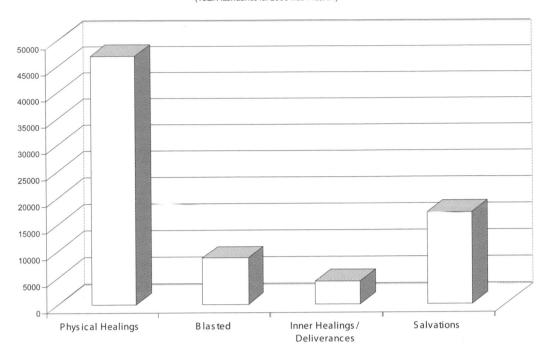

Statistics for 2006 B
(47,109 Physical Healings)

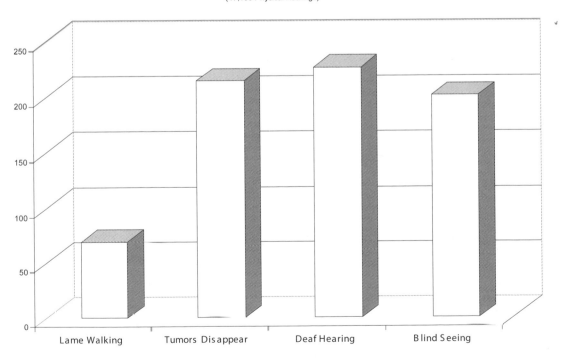

Statistics for 2007 A
(Total Attendance for 2007 was 274,671)

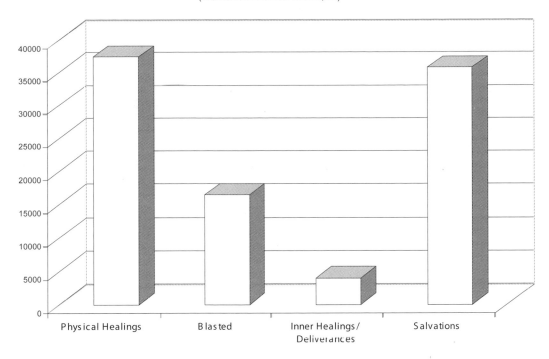

Statistics for 2007 B
(37,431 Physical Healings)

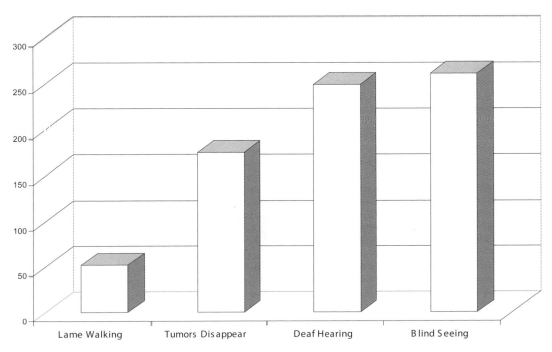

Final Statistics A

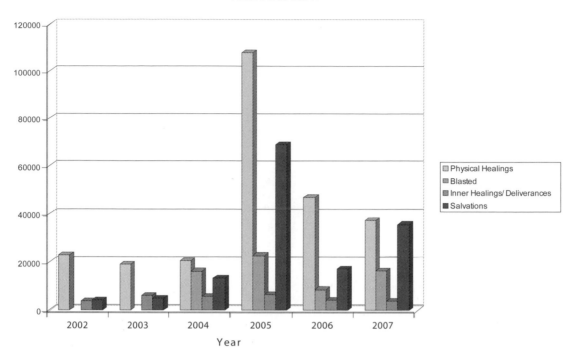

Final Statistics B

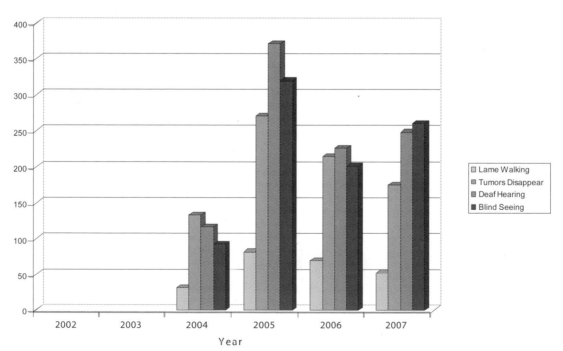

1. Vincent Synan, *In the Later Days: The Outpouring of the Holy Spirit in the Twentieth Century*. Revival Edition 2001, Xulan Press (Fairfax, VA 2001). p. 31.
2. ibid. p. 35.

Notes

Notes

Chapter 2: History of the Relationship between Church and the Medical Community

Lesson Goals

1) Introduce the reader to the history of health, healing, medicine, and views of life throughout the history of the church.
2) To look at how health and healing was viewed and perceived by the church.
3) This lecture is focused mainly on the establishment of the church after Jesus Christ came.

Introduction

We want to examine some of the history of the church and how it thought about health and healing, especially in its relationship to medicine and the medical profession. Throughout the church's history, it has mainly been positive toward medicine and doctors and rarely was it negative. Divine healing that comes supernaturally and naturalistic medicine are seen by the majority of the church as working hand in hand to bring health and healing to the individual person.

Key Insights

I) Jewish Understanding of the Body

A) Physical Body is Good

(1) Much of the ancient world viewed the body as bad - a prison for the soul.

B) Body is a vehicle used by God to carry out His purposes on the earth.

C) Physical Health of Utmost Importance

(1) According to the Talmudic rabbis, "it is forbidden to live in a city in which there is no physician," because doing so would expose a person's health to a major degree of risk and would prevent the person from fulfilling their responsibility to care for it (Kiddushin n.d.:66d).

(2) For early Judaism, things such as hygiene, diet, exercise, and sleep were not aspects of living properly, but were important religious duties.

(3) The story is told of Hillel, an important Jewish leader in the first century about how he tied religion and physical health together.
   a) "When he had finished the lesson with his students, he accompanied them part of the way. They said to him, "Master, where are you going?" "To perform a religious duty." "Which religious duty?" "To bathe in the bathhouse." "Is that a religious duty?" He answered them, "If somebody appointed to scrape and clean the statues of the king which are set up in the theaters and circuses is paid to do the work and furthermore associates with nobility, how much more so should I, who am created in the divine image and likeness, take care of my body!" (Leviticus Rabbah n.d.:34.3).

D) Physical Health and Serving God

   a) Maimonides (1135 - 1204) was a rabbi, a philosopher and a physician. He devoted much of his work to the theological motivation for serving God with our bodies. He said, "He who regulates his life in accordance with the laws of hygiene with the sole motive of maintaining a sound and vigorous physique and begetting children to do his work and labor for his benefit is not following the right course.

A man should aim to maintain a physical health and vigor in order that his soul may be upright, in a condition to know God...Whoever throughout his life follows this course will be continually serving God, even while engaged in business because and even during cohabitation, because his purpose in all that he does will be to satisfy his needs so as to have a sound body with which to serve God (M.T. Laws of Ethics n.d.:3.3).

E) There was No Dichotomy Between Spirit, Soul, Body

(1) Spirit, Soul, and Body were seen as affecting one another. Whatever they did in their spirit affected their body, and whatever they did with their physical body affected their spirit.

(2) George Eldon Ladd, New Testament Scholar, sums this concept up really well in his speaking of the OT view of life when he says, "There is no antithesis between physical and spiritual life, between the outer and inner dimensions in man, between the lower and higher realms. Life is viewed in its wholeness as the full enjoyment of God's gifts" (Ladd 1968:32).

II) Four Main Sources of Disease (Moving from the Jewish to the Christian understanding that developed from its Jewish roots.)

A) God Inflicts Disease because He is the Author of *Everything* – Sickness and Disease (This is the Old Testament viewpoint of the Sovereignty of God. The Old Testament has very little emphasis on the New Testament revelation of disease. However, the Old Testament has strong emphasis between disease and disobedience.)

> **Deuteronomy 32:39**
>
> See now that I myself am He!
> There is no god besides me.
> I put to death and I bring to life,
> I have wounded and I will heal,
> and no one can deliver out of my hand.

B) Demonic Causes

(1) There was a time, especially throughout the early church tradition, where demons and spirits were seen to be the main source and cause of sickness and disease. It was during this time period, in the words of one scholar, was "an age which was hag-ridden with fear of demonic forces dominating every aspect of life and death" (Frend 1965:356,548).

C) Sin in an Individual's Life

(1) This was reflected in the writings of such men as Thomas Beacon's (1512-1567) writings entitled **The Prayer for Them that are Sick**. He stated plainly that those who broke God's laws were visited with sickness and disease. This view was highly popular throughout the time of the Middle Ages. He was the Chaplain and Archbishop of Canterbury.

(2) The Jewish Talmud followed the same understanding when it said, "There is no suffering without iniquity" (Shabbat n.d.:55a).

D) Natural Causes

(1) The fact is that sometimes a person becomes sick because they haven't been eating the right type of

foods, getting enough rest, and taking care of their bodies.

(2) John Wesley emphasized that poor health habits often cause disease and good health habits could help prevent it.

(3) Ellen White and the Seventh Day Adventists emphasized this above all else. White's "dominant theme, especially after 1863, was that disease and suffering result from violations of divinely ordained physiological laws and are not the consequence of direct interventions from God. However, she frequently interpreted her family's mental and physical ailments as afflictions from Satan and his evil angels, who had made her and her husband 'the special objects" of their attention" (Numbers and Amundsen 1986:547).

III) Source of Suffering

A) Suffering is not Synonymous with physical sickness in the New Testament. Suffering, Biblically speaking, is usually referring to persecution.

B) Many have Interpreted Sickness as Suffering

(1) A tenth-century commentary put this in more graphic language when it said: "If a subject sins against his ruler, a blacksmith is commanded to fashion chains in which the ruler imprisons the sinner. When a man sins against the Lord, his limbs become his fetters" (Midrash Tadshe n.d.:16).

(2) Charles Spurgeon (1834-1892)
   a) He was not a stranger to suffering and suffered from a variety of sicknesses that made him take breaks from his pastoral ministry. He also had healings take place in some of his meetings.

   b) He said, "I venture to say that the greatest earthly blessing that God can give to any of us is health, with the exception of sickness. Sickness has frequently been of more use to the saints of God than health has...A sick wife, a newly made grave, poverty, slander, sinking of spirit, might teach us lessons nowhere else to be learned so well. Trials drive us to the realities of religion" (Spurgeon 1973:414).

(3) Pope Gregory I (540 - 604) in the Medieval Catholic Tradition
   a) In his pastoral handbook, wrote that "the sick are to be admonished so that they will feel that they are the sons of God because the scourge of discipline chastises them" (Gregory the Great n.d.:3.12).

C) Interpretation of Paul's Thorn in 2 Corinthians 12:7-10

(1) The typical Baptist position is held by John Gill (1697-1771), who was a pastor and professor of divinity.
   a) He believed that all human suffering stemmed from Adam's sin, which he called "the pandora from whence have sprung all spiritual maladies and bodily diseases; all the disasters, distresses, mischiefs, and calamities that are, or have been in the world" (Gill 1769:324).

   b) Human suffering is going to take place in every person. Because of the fall, the human race has become mortal and "it is liable ...to various diseases" (Gill 1769:342).

(2) Other scholars believe the thorn in the flesh is referring to persons or spirits who were opposing Paul. This is the meaning of the only other two references in the Bible, but in the Old Testament, to thorn in the flesh.

IV) James 5 and Its Effects Upon the Church

> **James 5:13-16**
> [13] Is any one of you in trouble? He should pray. Is anyone happy? Let him sing songs of praise. [14] Is any one of you sick? He should call the elders of the church to pray over him and anoint him with oil in the name of the Lord. [15] And the prayer offered in faith will make the sick person well; the Lord will raise him up. If he has sinned, he will be forgiven. [16] Therefore confess your sins to each other and pray for each other so that you may be healed. The prayer of a righteous man is powerful and effective. *(NIV)*

A) Early Catholicism

(1) Throughout early Catholicism there was the practice of anointing the sick with oil so they would be healed.

(2) There was a strong connection between the forgiveness of sins and the healing of physical sickness.

(3) In a letter by Pope Innocent I in the early fifth century, he addressed the use of anointed oil being used at home, which apparently was the way it was done.

(4) Causarius of Arles, in the early sixth century complaining about the sick people turning to pagan practices said, "How much more right and salutary it would be if they made haste to the church...and piously anointed themselves and their family with holy oil; and in accordance with the words of the Apostle James received not only health of the body but also pardon for their sins" (Poschmann n.d.:241-242).

(5) The laity began to practice anointing with oil. They would go from house to house and anoint with oil those who were sick that they might recover (The Early Middle Ages 500-1050) (Numbers and Amundsen 1986:80).

B) Extreme Unction

(1) "It became know in the tenth or eleventh century as Extreme Unction and for the most part lost any of its effective connection with physical healing..." (Numbers and Amundsen 1986:81).

(2) The Council of Trent in 1551 is where it became known as Extreme Unction.

(3) They called it Extreme Unction which was regarded by ancient tradition "as the completion not only of penance but also of the whole Christian life, which ought to be a continual penance" (Numbers and Amundsen 1986:114). It was used to prepare a person to pass from one life to the next.

   a) "This anointing is to be applied to the sick, but especially to those who are in such danger as to appear to be at the end of life, which is why it is also called the sacrament of the dying" (Numbers and Amundsen 1986:114).

C) Orthodox Tradition

(1) During the Byzantine period, in both east and west, oil was blessed for physical healing.

(2) East

   a) Gregory of Nazianzus, in his Theological Orations, suggests that Christians were to expect healing.

(3) West

    a) Pope Innocent I (416) described what seemed to be the norm in his letter when he wrote "the faithful who are sick can be anointed with the holy oil of unction, which has been prepared by the bishop and which not only priests but all Christians may use for anointing, when their own needs or those of their family demand" (Palmer 278).

(4) The Orthodox maintained the earlier tradition of the sacrament being a healing agent when the Roman Catholics changed it to Extreme Unction.

D) Calvinist Tradition

(1) The Calvinists rejected the anointing with oil because its use in the Catholic's Extreme Unction.

(2) Present day Presbyterians use it as long as the people being ministered to understand that it is not used with a medicinal purpose or as a substitute for medical care. They look at it in a purely symbolic way as God's redemptive purpose at work in their lives.

E) Modern Evangelicals

(1) Modern Evangelicals have usually interpreted the James 5 passage in a variety of ways. Let me just give you three of them here.

    a) The passage speaks of an apostolic rite that ceased with the passing of miracles.

    b) That it speaks of spiritual, not physical healing.

    c) That it offers a supernatural way of healing for those who are prayed over.

(2) Many, if not most, Evangelicals hold to the third view but they differ on what the purpose of the oil is.

    a) A.J. Gordon, who wrote much about healing, said it was representative of the Holy Spirit bringing healing to the body (Gordon n.d.:1).

    b) B.B. Warfield, on the other hand, who obviously was a cessationist, believed the oil was referring to medicinal means, and God was going to use available medicinal means to restore health (Warfield 1918:171-173).

(3) Because Evangelicals have never really rejected the use of medicine, they employ this rite as a last means when medicine has seemed to fail them.

F) Pentecostals

(1) Many Pentecostals use the means of James 5 to pray for physical healing today. They have always used the oil as a physical representation of the Holy Spirit.

G) Many Interpretations

(1) As we can see throughout the history of the church, there have been many interpretations of anointing with oil and praying for the sick.

(2) However the church has interpreted this passage, it can be clearly seen that it was used for the overall health and healing of the church.

(3) The early Church believed that the anointing that was in a person could be transferred to other things, like clothes taken from Paul in Acts 19, as well as water – when blessed became holy water, and oil when blessed or consecrated became holy oil – the oil of unction (unction = anointing or anointed). This

was especially true for oil because of James 5, it was a command of Scripture and was administered in faith with prayer. This understanding was and is also held by the Catholic and Orthodox Church today. Many Protestants also hold to this understanding of anointing oil. Protestants in Brazil bring clothes to the meetings to be prayed over, as is oil, to be prayed for by people they feel are anointed or holy people, Apostles, healing Evangelists, pastors.

V) Clergy Practice Medicine

A) There have been many clergy-physicians throughout the history of the church.

B) Pope Gregory I

(1) He was one of the most influential people in shaping early Catholic understanding. He put special emphasis on divine healing, demonology, the cult of the saints, and even on relics; however, he had a tremendous fascination with medicine.

(2) During this time it was not uncommon for the clerics to be seeking medical handbooks in their training and also giving much medical advice alongside their spiritual advice.

(3) Their understanding was that if God wants to touch a human being, He would help him through whatever he is going through.

(4) The Medieval Catholic Church didn't see a dichotomy between medical healing and spiritual healing. As we've seen previously and throughout this chapter, they were continually seen as coming from the hand of God.

(5) The Pope's fascination with medicine was still backed up by him reminding the people not to put their hope in drugs and remedies, but in God who is the ultimate healer.

(6) When one reads about physicians during this time period, there are only two classes of physicians: strictly secular physicians and cleric-physicians, who were almost always monks.

C) By the 12th century, medicine is taught in medical schools and is part of the education of the clergy.

D) Until well into the Renaissance (about 14th-17th Century), the doctor was also, generally speaking, the priest.

E) John Wesley

(1) Many of us know him by his intense preaching and the active part he played in the spread of Christianity throughout the United States. However, Wesley actively involved himself with the theory and practice of medicine throughout his life.

(2) John Wesley first began to read books about the "anatomy and physic medicine" shortly after entering Christ's Church College in Oxford University in 1721 at the age of seventeen. He continued to read such books in his leisure hours for 10 years.

(3) It was then that he studied medicine more seriously for several months in preparation for his and his brother Charles' missionary expedition to the New World colony of Georgia. He did this in order to "be

of some service to those who had no regular physician among them" (Wesley 1931:1.11,2.307).

(4) Such preparation was in keeping with the Anglican and Puritan tradition, which believed that preparation of this sort would enable ministers to contribute to the physical and spiritual well being of their parishioners in the absence of trained physicians.

(5) In 1747, Wesley published the first edition of **Primitive Physick**, which listed remedies for over 250 maladies and "contained a carefully constructed introduction about the history and theory of medicine, including a list of rules for maintaining health" (Numbers and Amundsen 1986:321). He would go on to write many more books such as **Thoughts on Nervous Disorders** (1784), and **The Duty and Advantage of Early Rising** (1789).

(6) Wesley has received much criticism for the things he wrote about medicine and healing during his time. Much of what he said was according to popular opinion of the time, not something that no one believed. "Compared to others, he wrote more plainly, generally prescribed less harsh, less complicated, and more readily available remedies, and simplified the organization of his book" (Numbers and Amundsen 1986:322).

(7) Wesley had a desire to bring caring and curing in body and spirit to those he ministered to. He did this by seeking God for spiritual matters but also tying together his love and knowledge of medicine to minister most effectively to people.

(8) Though some of the early Catholic ministers practiced medicine for monetary gain, Wesley always did it with a heart to bring health and healing to the people he loved and ministered to. There was not seen to be a conflict in interest between the medical profession and also the work of the clergy. Wesley had a heart to cut through the greed of the medical profession and return to the pure heart of why medicine was originally created – to help people who were created in God's image.

F) **Calvinistic Doctrines**

(1) Deacons have a specific role in medicine as attendants to the sick. They were to bring spiritual care as well as physical care for their sicknesses and diseases.

(2) Deaconnesses as well have a role in other protestant denominations. Hence "Deaconness Hospitals".

G) **Luke**

(1) From the earliest Christian days, it doesn't seem that the majority of Christians have been hostile in any way toward the medical professions and toward physicians.

(2) In fact, the Apostle Paul, who was used powerfully by God in divine healing, mentions Luke, "the beloved physician" (Col. 4:14), who wrote the book bearing his name and also the Book of Acts.

H) **The church never condemned the clergy-priest, just that theological study was much more important that physical for the priests.**

VI) **Positive View of Medicine**

A) **Even while Christians were establishing hospitals and caring for the sick in a naturalistic type of way, they were also going after divine healing and still claiming miraclous cures.**

B) Early Jewish Tradition

1) The early Jewish community believed in the importance of medicine and medical doctors throughout their history.

2) Ben Sira, who wrote in the third century B.C., that the new medical art and its practitioners were a fulfillment of God's will for them: "Honor a physician with the honor due to him for the uses which you may have of him, for the Lord created him…The Lord created medicines out of the earth, and he who is wise will not abhor them" (Ecclesiasticus n.d.:38:1-12).

C) Eastern Orthodox Tradition

(1) In the later Jewish deuterocanonical writings, the healing power of God is exalted above medical practices: "For it was neither herb, nor mollifying plaster that restored them to health: by thy word, O Lord, which healeth all things. For thou hast the power of life and death" (Wis. 16:12-13) (Brenton 1851). In the Eastern Orthodox tradition, you can see the positive relationship between medicine and prayer.

(2) However, the physician was to be honored, "for the Lord has created him." (Eccl. 38:1).

(3) Prayer to God and going to a physician were not contradictory in terms, but they were to be supplementary practices, providing the normative foundation for faith and medicine.

(4) This is illustrated in Ecclesiasticus 38:9-15:
   a) My son, in thy sickness be not negligent: but pray to the Lord, and he will make thee whole. Leave off from sin, and order thy hands aright, and cleanse thy heart from all wickedness. Give sweet savour, and a memorial of fine flour; and make a fat offering. Then give place to the physician, for the Lord hath created him: let him not go from thee, for thou hast need of him. There is a time when in their hands there is good success. For they shall also pray unto the Lord, that he would prosper that which they give for ease and remedy to prolong life. He that sinneth before his Maker, let him fall into the hands of the physician.

(5) Coptic-Orthodox Christianity

   a) The Coptic Orthodox Church of Alexandria is the official name of the largest Christian church in Egypt. It belongs to the Oriental Orthodoxy family of churches, which is distinctly different from Eastern Orthodoxy or Western churches.

   b) The foundation of the church is in Egypt, but the Coptic Orthodox Church (literally the *Egyptian Orthodox Church*) maintains a worldwide following.

   c) Beliefs on Divine Healing
      Demonstrated in the following:
      - Prayer
      - Anointing by priests
      - Icons
      - "Unction"
      - Visitations by saints
      - Miracle-workers

"While many other religious denominations today believe that the healing miracles of the Lord Jesus Christ have somehow passed away, **our beloved Orthodox Church has held fast to the belief in 'healings' throughout its more than 2000 years of Coptic Christianity. Furthermore, the writings of the early church fathers document and speak often of the healing miracles within the church**" (Youssef 2002: Para.5)

d) Many early saints credited as being blessed to heal the sick, or perform signs and wonders
   - St. Demiana
   - Maximus and Domatius
   - St. Nicholas

e) Origen (AD 185-284) was the first of the early church fathers to suggest a decrease in supernatural ministry in the church.
   - He claims that it is the "lack of holiness and purity among the Christians of his day as the reason" (Hyatt 2002:20)

f) Icons
   - St. Mina's Clay Bottles

g) Practice of divine healing in modern times.
   - Anba Abraam – 1896 Cholera epidemic
   - Ewing's Sarcoma – 1994 healing at Al-Muqattam

D) Early Church Fathers' Attitude Toward Medicine and Doctors

(1) If you examine the early church fathers, you will find that not many of them were hostile toward the secular medical profession.
   a) Clement of Alexandria (155-220) spoke of it as God's gift to the human race that was discovered by reason.
   b) Origen (185-254) referred to medicine as "beneficial and essential to mankind."
   c) John Chrysostom (344/354-407) acknowledged physicians and medicine as gifts of God.

   d) Basil the Great (330-379) wrote to his fellow monks regarding medicine and the medical arts: "We must take great care to employ this medical art, if it should be necessary, not as making it wholly accountable for our state of health or illness, but as redounding to the glory of God…In the event that medicine should fail to help, we should not place all hope for the relief of our distress in this art…Yet, to reject entirely the benefits to be derived from this art is the sign of a pettish nature…We should neither repudiate this art altogether nor does it behoove us to repose all our confidence in it…When reason allows, we call in the doctor, but we do not leave off hoping in God" (Amundsen 1996:338-339).

   e) The relationship between the church and medical world was very favorable, at least through the 4th century.

E) Catholics, Roman Catholics, Anglicans, Lutherans, Methodists

(1) Many in the earlier traditions didn't have a distinction between divine healing and healing which comes through medical means. They believed that if God healed with anything but divine intervention, then it was a gift from God. In the same way, if medical means was used to heal, they saw that as a gift from God, as well, because God gave them wisdom on how to produce the medical means.

(2) Physicians were consulted because they functioned as part of God's partners in treatment, not someone who was being a substitute for God.

(3) They saw divine healing and medicinal healing coming from the hand of God and bringing health and healing to the individual person.

VII) Negative Views of Medicine within the church

A) Seventh Day Adventist (Formally established in 1863).

(1) Beginning of the Adventists: they had a negative view of modern medicine and doctors.

(2) They focused on using water and other natural remedies.

(3) Ellen White shows her belief in medicine being evil when she says, "I was shown that more deaths have been caused by drug-taking than from all other causes combined. If there was in the land one physician in the place of thousands, a vast amount of premature mortality would be prevented" (Numbers and Amundsen 1986:451).

(4) White was a semi-invalid for years. She taught her disciples to have nothing to do with physicians: "If any among us are sick, let us not dishonor God by applying to earthly physicians, but apply to the God of Israel. If we follow his directions (Jas. 5:14, 15) the sick will be healed. God's promise cannot fail. Have faith in God, and trust wholly in him."

(5) She later softened her stand when in 1860 she wrote "in some cases the counsel of an earthly physician is very necessary."

(6) Adventists live an average of 7 years longer than most in the United States of America because of their healthful lifestyle.

B) Primitive Pentecostals

(1) One particular Pentecostal proudly explained that "instead of trying to fight disease by means of doctors, drugs and human resources…our people rebuke and cast out demons" (Numbers and Amundsen 1986:523).

(2) Lillian Yeomans summed up the Pentecostal position when she said, "Therefore, not healing only, but absolute immunity from disease is ours in Christ Jesus" (Yeomans 1926:46).

(3) They, together with the Faith Cure movement, brought a renewed emphasis on divine healing to the Body of Christ.

(4) A large minority acknowledged medical care was an inferior, yet morally permissible alternative for Christians with weak faith.

C) Modern Day Pentecostals

(1) Oral Robert's City of Faith Medical and Research Center started in Tulsa in 1978.

(2) They had graduate schools in medicine, dentistry, and nursing; a thirty story hospital, and a laboratory specializing in aging, cancer, and heart disease. They had to close it down in 1989 due to financial reasons.

(3) Holistic view of health is shown in the University's motto: "To educate the whole man in spirit, mind and body."

VIII) Building of Hospitals

A) Christians' Intense Love for Sick People

(1) Medical historian Roy Porter says, "Charity was the supreme religious virtue. In the name of love, and with the conviction that every human was a soul to be saved, believers were enjoined to care for those in need: the destitute, the handicapped, the poor, the hungry, those without shelter, and perhaps above all, the sick" (Porter 1993:1452).

(2) It has been suggested that it was the Christians who began the hospitals because they cared for the sick. They played a very important role in the founding of hospitals. (Important to note that due to the development of hospitals there began a decrease in faith for divine healing.)

(3) It was the early Christians who concerned themselves with the sick long before there were institutions to do so.

(4) Dionysius (ca. 264) was bishop of the city of Alexandria. He talked about the differing attitudes and behaviors of the pagans and Christians in the face of disaster. He said, "The most of our brethren were unsparing in their exceeding love and brotherly kindness. They held fast to each other and visited the sick fearlessly, and ministered to them continually, serving them in Christ. And they died with them most joyfully, taking the affliction of others, and drawing the sickness from their neighbors to themselves and willingly receiving their pains. And many who cared for the sick and gave strength to others died themselves, have transferred to themselves their death....Truly the best of our brethren departed from life in this manner, including some presbyters and deacons and those of the people who had the highest reputation; so that this form of death, through the great piety and strong faith it exhibited, seemed to lack nothing of martyrdom" (Shaff and Wace 1979:307).

(5) In 534, St. Benedict of Nursia wrote "The Rule of St. Benedict." Written to the monks, in the eighth century becomes the central monastic rule in the west. According to this rule, all monks and nuns are resolved to love and serve the sick. (Pollak 1963:79).

B) Establishment of Medical Practices

(1) The Christian belief that humans were created in God's image gave rise to the establishment of the medical practice. It was the Christian concern for all persons, even those who were sick, which led to the establishment of the first hospitals in Western Civilization in the 4th century.

(2) In this time, pagans didn't care for their sick in any organized way or on a widespread basis. The Church, however, offered not only care to Christians, but also to non-Christians.

(3) Basil the Great established the first great hospital in Asia Minor around 370.
   a One of the earliest and best well known, was the Basileias, which was founded in 372 by Basil the Great. The hospital had both nurses and medical attendants. Gregory of Nazianzus (330-389), who had been to those type of hospitals, described it in very passionate terms: "Go forth a little from the city, and behold a new city, the treasure-house of godliness…in which disease is investigated and sympathy proved. …We have no longer to look on the fearful and pitiable sight of men like corpses

before death, whit the greater part of their limbs dead [from leprosy], driven from cities, from dwellings, from public places, from watercourses…Basil it was more than anyone who persuaded those who are men not to scorn men, nor to dishonor Christ the head of all by their inhumanity towards human beings" (Smith and Cheetham 1875:786).

b) Basil's hospitals provided a model that spread throughout the Roman Empire in the fifth century. Pagans usually recognized hospitals as purely Christian during this time period.

(4) Augustine presents a perspective on secular medicine that is very positive. At the same time, the practice of medicine is seen as "material evidence of God's love and compassion for human suffering" (Amundsen 1982:349).

(5) Many clergy-operated monasteries were operated as the primary institutions for healing. In Europe, hospitals were "usually associated with a church or monastery, with religion defining life within them" (Bynun and Porter 1993:1182).

(6) Many of the Christian denominations and traditions had a desire to reach out to the poor and sick in order to take care of them and that is how the first hospitals were formed.

IX) The Problem with Dogma

A) Christian dogma slows down medical progress in the late Middle Ages.

B) Scientific dogma (not the Scientific Method) today is slowing down medical progress. Especially the older view of the human body as a machine.

C) Hopefully, we are entering a stage where truth rather than dogma will unite the medical and spiritual professionals.

P.T. *Kiddushin* 66d; see also B.T. *Sanhedrin* 17b. as quoted in *Caring and Curing*, Numbers and Amundsen ed., (John Hopkins University Press, 1986).

Ibid. Leviticus Rabbah 34.3.

Ibid. M.T. *Laws of Ethics* 3.3; see also 4:1.

The Pattern of New Testament Truth, George Eldon Ladd, (William B. Eerdmans Publishing Co., Grand Rapids, Mich., 1968) p. 32.

See W.H.C. Frend, *Martydom and Persecution in the Early Church* (Oxford, 1965), pp. 356, 548.

Ibid. *Shabbat* 55a; see also *Sanhedrin* 101a.

Edited by Numbers and Amundsen, *Caring and Curing*, (Johns Hopkins University Press, 1986), pp 457.

Ibid. *Midrash Tadshe* 16.

C.H. Spurgeon, *Autobiography*, 2 Vols. (Edinburgh, 1973), 2:414.

Gregory the Great, *Regula Pastoralis* 3.12.

John Gill, *The Body of Divinity* (London [1769] 1839), p. 324.

Gill, Ibid. 342.

Caesarius of Arles, *Sermon* 279.5, quoted by Poschmann, *Penance*, pp.241-242.

Caring and Curing, p. 80.

Caring and Curing, p 81.

Caring and Curing, p 114.

Henry Denzinger, *Enchiridion Symbolorum Definitionum et Declarationum de rebus Fidei et Morum*, 28th (Freiburg, 1952), pp. 321-323. Quoted Caring and Curing, p 114. by *Caring and Curing* pg. 114.

References to be found in Palmer, *Sacraments and Forgiveness*, pg. 278

See A.J. Gordon, *The Ministry of Healing* (Harrisburg, PA), pg 1.

See B.B. Warfield, *Counterfeit Miracles* (1918, reprinted London, 1972), pp 171-173.

John Wesley, *The Letters of the Reverend John Wesley*, ed. John Telford, 8 vols. (London, 1931), 1:11, 2:307.

Caring and Curing, pg. 321.

Caring and Curing, pg. 322

Ecclesiasticus 38:1-12.

Deuterocanonical quotations are from *The Septuagint Version of the Old Testament and Apocrypha*, trans. Sir Launcelot Lee Brenton (London, 1851; reprinted Grand Rapids, MI, 1980).

The Long Rule 55. Quoted in Amundsen, "Medicine and Faith," pp. 338-339.

Caring and Curing, pg. 451

Caring and Curing, pg. 523

Lillian Yeomans, M.D., *Healing from Heaven* (Springfield, MO, 19260, p. 46.

Porter, R. (1993). Religion and Medicine. In W.F. Bynum & R. Porter (eds.), *Companion Encyclopedia of the History of Medicine*. New York: Routledge, Chapman, & Hall. pg. 1452.

Eusebius, *Church History*, Book VII< ch. 23 in *The Nicene and Post-Nicene Fathers*, eds. Philip Schaff and Henry Wace (Grand Rapids, MI, 1979) 2nd Series, Vol. 1, p. 307

Pollak, K. (1963). *The Healers: The Doctor, Then and Now*. Camden, N.J. : Thomas Nelson and Sons. Pg. 79

Oration 20. Quoted by W. smith and S. Cheetham, *A Dictionary of Christian Antiquities*, vol. 1 (London, 1875), s.v. "Hospitals," p. 786.

Amundsen, D.W. (1982). Medicine and faith in early Christianity. *Bulletin of the History of Medicine*, 56, 326-350, pg. 349.

Granshaw, L., (1993). The hospital. In W.F. Bynum & R. Porter (eds.), *Companion Encyclopedia of the History of Medicine*. New York: Routledge, Chapman, & Hall, pg. 1182.

Chapter 3: Health and Wellness: Causes of Illness

Lesson Goals

1) Review the need for collaboration between medical or therapy treatment models and divine healing
2) Compare the taking of a medical history to the interview done in a healing model
3) Learn how specific illnesses have been prayed for by those with extensive experience in healing prayer

Introduction

In this section we are reminded that there are many avenues to maintaining good health. Besides maintenance through healthy lifestyles, Christians also have the gift of healing. By looking at how a physician approaches a complete medical history, we can gain understanding on how various organs and systems can receive healing as we pray for the whole person.

Key Insights

I) Health and wellness is a large topic, and may require a textbook and four years of post graduate education. But we can look at an overview for the purposes of a school of healing that compares medical and spiritual perspectives on a Christian model of healing for the whole person. A whole seminar could be developed on alternative therapies or complementary medicine, and how to integrate that into the healing process. Another seminar could be developed on food, nutritional supplements, vitamins, and proper fluid balance. Also a topic like proper exercise, and proper balance of rest, work, and recreation would be good. But since the scope of one lecture could get too large, we will leave it up to each person to pray for wisdom in these matters, and seek wise counsel from Christian leaders or professionals in these fields.

A) Healing ministry and medical or therapeutic professions are not exclusive of each other. They are complementary, not antagonistic. The focus here will be on divine health for the spirit, soul, and body, not on illness. After all, disease is just the lack of ease, not resting in our inheritance of complete health. It may often be related to not living out of our spirit, not drawing on His Presence continually. ***In Him was life, and the life was the light of men***, John 1:3, NKJV. This implies that if we live in the light of His Presence continually, and have our spirit draw on His Spirit for every thought, then we would see divine health and life each moment in our lives and ministries. It seems all of the great mystics of the church were continually seeking to have their spirit one with Him, that His thoughts would become their thoughts.

B) Every now and then a news report states that some ministry told an adult or child to go off their medications or insulin or other treatments, then serious injury or death resulted. This is a very irresponsible act, and no one should ever be told to go off their medications. While it is true we may be praying for divine healing, the only safe advice is to continue to work closely with your doctor or caregiver and follow his or her advice. In the normal course of many illnesses, there can be improvements that may warrant a reduction or gradual discontinuation of some medications, so doctors will know when it is safe or appropriate to make adjustments in the treatments or medications. But the prayer ministry should stay out of the way, and respect the professional boundaries. This is true even when medical professionals are serving in a prayer ministry; at that point they are acting as ministers, and they may need to remind the person that they are not acting as medical professionals.

C) The medical profession has looked askance at healing ministry because at times outlandish claims or testimonials are advertised, without adequate medical documentation. It is better to have fewer testimonies with less hype and more documentation, than the other extreme of overstatement in multiple testimonies, even though they may come from well-meaning people who just aren't sure what they are saying.

D) For this reason Randy's talks in Healing School I are very important: "The Thrill of Victory," and "The Agony of Defeat."

E) From the other direction, healing ministries have too often seen the medical and surgical treatment team as their adversaries, when such is not the case. A large number of professionals from various fields are Christians who will be open to healing prayer as an adjunct, even if they are not involved in an active healing ministry themselves.

F) One avenue to better understanding would be for us to design and complete some large scale studies on divine healing, probably with help from Christians who do research at medical universities.

II) When praying for health and wellness, we have been taught in the School of Healing and Impartation to start with the interview, much like taking a medical history. Let's look at how a medical history is taken:

A) First is the chief complaint, or, "What is the problem?" It is important to hear about the person's problem in their own words, not your immediate diagnostic impression. You may need to repeat the statement back to them, to be sure you heard them correctly.

B) The next section is the history of the present illness, where you might ask what first brought on the problem, what makes it better or worse. You may ask if it has been diagnosed and treated, and in what way. If you sense it is a serious problem you can encourage them to consult a doctor, or go to an emergency room immediately if it is something like chest pain.

C) After the present history the doctor will usually ask about past medical history, developmental problems, trauma, or surgery. Any time where there was a poor result or an accident the person may need to offer a prayer of forgiveness for the caregiver during the interview. There is nothing that will block healing like unforgiveness. Besides, if the present problem gets healed, one or two of the old problems might come up again for healing as the person's level of faith increases.

D) After past history the diagnostic interview goes on to family history, social history, spiritual history, and review of systems. Family history is especially important if you are alert to the possibility of generational curses. In the social history you might want to know about their family of origin, where they came in the birth order, their current relationships, and work. In the spiritual history you can ask when they became a believer, have they been filled with His Spirit, what is His call on their life, and what gifts and fruit they see. I especially focus on their identity as sons and daughters. I ask have they been baptized in the Father's love?

E) The review of systems is best remembered by visualizing the person from their head to their feet. In the next section we will review the body and organ systems from head to feet as a way of evaluating their current needs, and developing a strategy for healing prayer.

III)   The review of systems is a way of remembering all the areas where there may be a problem, and also a way of remembering about different disease processes. For more information on how to pray for the spiritual roots behind specific diseases, you may want to consult a workbook sold at The Global Awakening resource table: *Healing Rooms: Healing for Specific Diseases.* This comes from Cal Pierce and the Healing Rooms Ministry. It is an excellent resource.

A) Head. Actually, this will include head, eyes, ears, nose, and throat. Was there trauma to the head or brain? Is there a disease of the scalp or face? Any problem with vision, pain in the eyes, or alignment of the eyes? Headaches, like migraines, are common and frequently respond to prayer. If they keep their head down, remind them that Jesus is the lifter of their head. Problems in the ear include chronic infections that may have ruptured the eardrum, frozen the bones of hearing in the middle ear, caused deafness, or vertigo if the inner ear was affected. A deaf and dumb spirit may need to be cast out. Vertigo may be from witchcraft. God is not the author of confusion but of peace. Nose and sinus problems are often obstructions to breathing, and they need the fresh air of heaven to come and purify their airways. Allergic reactions to pollen or dust may trigger sinusitis, and when we see the allergic response going off too frequently, causing disease, we often think about strongholds of fear. This is a good time to break the stronghold of fear before continuing to pray for the healing. We know that perfect love casts out all fear.

B) Neck problems may include swallowing problems in the back of the throat or in the esophagus. There may be tumors. Rarely, but more often there is constriction or inflammation from reflux esophagitis, too much acid and a valve mechanism that doesn't work properly. This can be related to unresolved anger that had to be "swallowed," which results in bitterness. A stronghold of bitterness and unforgiveness must often be broken before the complete healing comes. Sometimes people have trouble with vocal cords, and cannot speak properly. There may again be a spirit of intimidation or fear that needs to be broken. Severe choking spells can be a sign that in the generations there was some involvement with freemasonry. Another situation is when the person tells you they have thyroid problems or you can see a goiter. Thyroid inflammation starts off these problems, and thyroiditis is often an autoimmune disease, related to self hatred and a stronghold of rejection.

C) Chest problems. This might include chest wall and rib pain, breast tumors, lung problems, and heart disease. Breast tumors can sometimes be from a generational curse, especially if there is a need for forgiveness between mother and daughter. Asthma and wheezing, like sinus allergies, can be related to a stronghold of fear, so you may need to look for early traumas. Heart disease can be related to chronic fears also, but some cardiovascular diseases, like hypertension, can be linked to simmering anger and resentments.

D) Stomach and abdominal problems. Peptic ulcers and esophagitis (gastroesophageal reflux disease, GERD) are also related to anger, resentments and unforgiveness. Tumors and cancers in general can be related to hopelessness, a feeling of being doomed by a curse. Diabetes is a malfunction of the islet cells in the pancreas that no longer put out insulin. It may be a generational curse of self hatred, of words spoken against themselves by previous generations. Liver disease can be related to the damage caused by addictions and alcoholism. The shame may need to be lifted off the person. Cirrhosis can be one of the generational curses of freemasonry. Crohn's Disease and ulcerative colitis are autoimmune diseases of the bowel and may be related to self-rejection. But sometimes the immune system is not protecting a person because it is "asleep," which may mean they also have a slumbering spirit, not yet awakened to their destiny, or a sense that they were not wanted.

E) The back can have multiple problems like old fractures, osteoporosis and collapsed vertebrae, disc herniations, spinal stenosis, kyphosis, lordosis, and scoliosis. Alignment and scoliosis seem to lift when you speak in the authority of the Lord Jesus, to line up to your purposes and destiny. Like all healings, it seems to flow most easily when His Presence is strong, when there has been a word of knowledge and you are flowing in the anointing. Serious problems of the back can sometimes be related to a need for healing the relationship with the father or mother, with more forgiveness and honoring.

F) Pelvic area and reproduction. Problems like ovarian cysts and pelvic pain may be attempts of the enemy to cause infertility. Even if they are curses from witchcraft, a blessing can reverse the curse, and allow the person to be fruitful and multiply. Early traumas may need to be healed, such as words that told the person they would have no future generations.

G) Extremities. Next come the legs and arms and all the joints. Some of the arthritis problems are autoimmune diseases, and may need a healing of self-hatred or of bitterness before the physical healing. Varicose veins cause blockage of the veins and the valves in them are not opening properly. This may cause painful swelling and blood clots. A word of blessing or release can open up this blockage. A similar process occurs when we pray to open up an area where the arterial blood flow has been blocked by disease. If we hold our hands on a cool area until we start to feel warmth and color change, then pronounce the blessing we will often see dramatic healing. A pastor in Mozambique told Randy and a Global Awakening team he uses this technique when praying for the dead, whose feet are obviously cold, and stay that way, unless the Lord is about to raise the dead!

H) Skin problems include eczema, psoriasis, acne, rosacea, and results of burns or trauma leaving scars. In the recent revival many scars are disappearing which means we can expect more. The Spirit of Christ Jesus flows, by the washing of the water of the Word, to cleanse any defilement or disfigurement off the beloved Bride. When you sense His compassion, healing often follows.

I) Mental health is addressed in the session on inner healing.

IV) In this overview of healing the physical body, we don't want to leave an impression that we use a cookbook approach to each person. The Holy Spirit may give unique guidance and instruction in each situation. Furthermore, there is often emotional healing and spiritual impartation or deliverance going on at the same time as physical healing. In a church that stresses communion as a holy sacrament, healing in all these areas flows more easily during and after communion. But even in churches that would say they do not stress these things as sacraments, still the times of anointing with oil, times when a spirit of forgiveness and repentance is strong, when there has been communion and a spirit of unity in the church, then all these prayers for healing seem to operate more fully. The glory Presence of Christ Jesus in His Spirit produces unity, righteousness, peace and joy that are foundations for healing.

Psalm 16:11

"In your Presence is fullness of joy and at your right hand there are pleasures forevermore."

It is our desire to bring all people into His Glory Presence and abide there as a permanent habitation, where divine health also abides permanently.

Chapter 4: Psychoneuroimmunology and Healing

Lesson Goals

1) Introduce the student to the immune system as a wall of protection, much like the walls of a city in the Bible.
2) Identify specific cells and their function in the immune system, and see how faith enhances their function.
3) Review how the immune system can restore and renew while it fights off disease, much like the Spirit in us.

Introduction

In this section we can see once again how we are fearfully and wonderfully made when we review the amazing immune system. When researchers began to see how the brain, the mind, and the immune system were inter-related, the field of psychoneuroimmunology was born. But we know that faith and the spiritual life also enhance immune function, and we will look at research in this area.

Key Insights

I) The immune system is equivalent to watchmen on the wall, and also a sign that the Lord gave provision for self-healing in the spirit, soul, and body.

A) We are a city set on a hill.

> **Matthew 5:14**
>
> [14]You are the light of the world. A city that is set on a hill cannot be hidden. (NKJV)

B) A city has foundations, outer walls, inner walls and towers to defend it, along with watchmen on the wall. The immune system has multiple layers. Some are static barriers and some are active defenses, the adaptive immune system.

C) The Presence of the Lord Jesus Christ through His Spirit is our foundation.

> **Isaiah 28:16**
>
> Behold, I lay in Zion a stone for a foundation, A tried stone, a precious cornerstone, a sure foundation. (NKJV)

D) When our innermost person, our spirit, has built its foundation or identity with Christ, then we know we are true sons and daughters of God, and we have received the same blessing of the Father through the Spirit that Jesus received.

> **Matthew 3:17**
>
> This is my beloved Son, in whom I am well pleased. (NKJV)

E) The walls of the city are built from living stones, because they are active and increasing in size. The kingdom of God within each person and within the entire Church is increasing, and the walls are expanding. Our immune system, like our entire person, can be infused with divine health.

F) The immune system has trouble maintaining health when people are continually in stress, but when they are at rest in their identity as sons and daughters, then the river of His peace and joy flows out of their innermost person.

> **John 7:38**
>
> 38 He who believes in Me, as the Scripture has said, out of his heart will flow rivers of living water.

> **Psalm 46:4**
>
> 4 *There is* a river whose streams shall make glad the city of God,
>   The holy *place* of the tabernacle of the Most High.

G) One thing that happens during chronic stress is that CRH (corticotrophin releasing hormone) in the mid-brain gets the message from the DNA to upregulate, which then upregulates ACTH (adrenocorticotropic hormone) in the pituitary, then finally increasing cortisol in the adrenal gland. The genetic code gives the instructions when to upregulate or downregulate a system. We know digital data can be uploaded or downloaded from the internet to your computer. But can healing power in the Spirit be uploaded or downloaded?

> **Luke 8:46**
>
> 46 But Jesus said, "Somebody touched Me, for I perceived power going out from Me." (NKJV).

These are downloads; one day the Lord gave me instruction on uploads as well.

II) Watchmen on the wall are referenced in Isaiah 62:6,7 and 11,12 (NKJV):

> 6 I have set watchmen on your walls, O Jerusalem
>
> They shall never hold their peace day or night.
>
> You who make mention of the Lord, do not keep silent.
>
> 7 And give Him no rest till He establishes
>
> And till He makes Jerusalem a praise in the earth…
>
> 11 Indeed the Lord has proclaimed to the end of the world:
>
> Say to the daughter of Zion, "Surely your salvation is coming;
>
> Behold His reward is with Him, and His work before Him."
>
> 12 And they shall call them The Holy People, the Redeemed of the Lord;
>
> And you shall be called Sought Out, A City Not Forsaken.

A) Notice the watchmen have to be vigilant; they shall never hold their peace day or night. The immune system must have enough reserve (watchmen) and they must be alert and well rested to remain vigilant.

B) We defend the city and the kingdom, so we can win for the Lamb the reward He is due. Then he comes for His Bride, the daughter of Zion, as in verse 11 above.

C) Another result of turning to the Lord for His protection is that the stronghold of rejection or forsakenness is broken, as in verse 12 above. This is one of the most persistent assaults against the city walls, from the accuser of the brethren. He continually says to the church, "You are forsaken." But the Lord Himself says, "I will never leave you nor forsake you." He is our Advocate. He calls us His Beloved, Sought Out.

D) My wife, Lorraine, had an interesting experience with the Lord Jesus as her Advocate, when they faced the accusers one day in the second heavens where these accusations are made.

III) If there is an illness due to infection, cancer or trauma, the immune system and reparative cells can restore the body, mind, and spirit to health. Repair and restoration is a sign of the kingdom, and believers can receive it as part of their inheritance.

A)

> **Isaiah 58:12**
>
> [12]Those from among you shall build the old waste places; you shall raise up the foundations of many generations; and you shall be called the Repairer of the Breach, the Restorer of Streets to Dwell In. (NKJV)

B) Repair and restoration in the central nervous system used to be unthinkable, but now we know there is such a thing as neural plasticity, and there is a protein molecule called Brain-Derived Neurotrophic Factor (BDNF).

C) Depression and aging lower the levels of BDNF. The area of the brain called the hippocampus, where memory is organized, is sensitive to BDNF, to substance P and to cortisol, a stress hormone that is at higher levels in chronic anxiety and chronic depression.

D) There is another area of the brain called the amygdala, where emotional memory is organized. Amygdala means almond in Greek, and the two amygdalas are the shape of almonds, found bilaterally in the midbrain. We know that chronic stress as in post traumatic stress disorder or in depression leaves the body with levels of cortisol that are too high, and this will eventually cause the cells in the amygdala to atrophy. But with healing of the traumatic memories and recovery of depression the cortisol will go down, and the prayer minister can call up the restorative properties (BDNF), to start the healing process.

E) Amygdala-tree in Greek is the Shakedh-tree in Hebrew, which means the Hasty-tree.

> **Jeremiah 1:11-12**
>
> [11]Moreover the word of the Lord came to me, saying, "Jeremiah, what do you see?" And I said, "I see a branch of an almond tree." [12]Then the Lord said to me, "You have seen well, for I am ready to perform My word."

The rod of an almond tree budded the earliest, and this also may have been Aaron's rod that budded. The idea is that the Lord will hasten to perform His word. But in our brains the amygdala may be too hasty and also too loud, drowning out more calm reasoning. It is possible for a prayer minister to speak to the amygdala, to tell it to slow down, to quiet down, and come into balance with the rest of the brain.

F) One preliminary study I found suggested that a health food like soy or tofu may actually lower the levels of BDNF in men. They were calling it soy dementia!

IV) Some components of the immune system include lymphocytes, neutrophils, natural killer cells, and several chemical reactions called cytokines, enkephalins, complement, and beta defensins.

A) A cytokine called interleukin-1 plays multiple roles within the brain, including inducing "sickness behavior" (sleepiness, anorexia, fatigue). Recovery from infection may be aided by "listening" to one's immune system's effects on the brain. Interestingly, the word "rapha" in Hebrew can mean be still, be sick, faint, or get well, but it first means "Be still and know that I am God," Psalm 46:10.

B) A cytokine called interleukin-6 plays a role in acute inflammatory response, proliferation of B cells, and it is elevated in the elderly with chronic diseases. (To read more on interleukins and faith, see The Link Between Religion and Health—Psychoneuroimmunology and the Faith Factor, by Koenig and Cohen, pp 37-38.)

C) While some parts of the immune response are passive defenses, other parts, called the adaptive immune system, are quite active in seeking out the offending agent, to destroy it. This would be like reinforcements streaming out of the tower, in full armor, as an offense rather than a defense.

Proverbs 18:10

[10]The name of the Lord is a strong tower; the righteous run in to it and they are saved. (NKJV)

D) The immune system keeps a watch or surveillance for cancer cells, and is continually removing them before they get established. But the immune system can also help rid the body of cancer once it starts growing. The type of lymphocytes in this process are called natural killer cells. Levy and colleagues reported this in 1991 in their study of 90 women recently diagnosed with stage 1 or stage 2 cancer. Higher natural killer activity during recovery and at follow-up visits predicted more disease-free survival in the cases studied. In another study reported by Schall and colleagues at Stanford in 1998, 112 women with metastatic breast cancer, who were in treatment, were evaluated for natural killer cell activity and also cortisol levels as a measure of stress hormones, and those who said they relied on their spiritual expression for strength had much higher levels of natural killer cells and activity. They also had lower levels of evening cortisol, showing less stress in general.

E) It is amazing to me that at a time forty years ago, a person was adversely affected by an allergen that was only one part per billion in the air, and yet the moment the body comes in contact with that allergen again, the immune response swings into full gear. This shows the amazing memory of the T cell lymphocytes, among other things. We need to have a memory that scans the emotional atmosphere and also the spiritual atmosphere that says, "Wait a minute, I have heard that deception before. To arms, to arms!"

V) Other components include the natural barriers of the skin and mucous membranes.

A) We don't need to train our body to have these natural barriers to disease, but we do need to train our minds to have barriers to negative thoughts that may produce mental and physical illness.

B)

> **I Peter 5:8**
>
> [8]Be sober, be vigilant, because your adversary the devil walks about like a roaring lion, seeking whom he may devour. (NKJV)

C) The skin and the mucous membranes can be trained to allow the healing light of His glory Presence to pass through, as when He breathes air into the room around someone with a respiratory illness, or when you feel the heat during the laying on of hands.

D) When you envision the multiple layers or walls of immunity meant to protect the body, I also think of the spiritual walls we have been given to protect our own spirit from the world, from the evil one. In her classic book, The Interior Castle, St. Teresa of Avila tells of the vision she was given by God. She saw the spirit of a person as a celestial ball, an orb, which was their castle. There were seven layers; you could live at the outer rooms which were in contact with the world and the evil one, or you could learn to travel through the levels to the innermost room, where His Majesty, the Lord Jesus Christ, sits in glory on His throne. That is where the real strength comes, to supply all the outer defenses. In His Presence is fullness of joy, and at His right hand are pleasures forevermore.

> **Psalm 16:11**
>
> [11]You will show me the path of life;
> In Your presence *is* fullness of joy;
> At Your right hand *are* pleasures forevermore. (NKJV)

VI) When the person's immune system has not been protecting them, they may become subject to repeated infections, degenerative illnesses, or cancer. The spirit within a person may be slumbering when it should be awake; this is happening while the immune system is underactive and the body is getting sick. One thing the prayer minister can do is to call the person's spirit to awaken and also speak life into the immune system.

A) Reasons for the spirit to be slumbering can include depression, fatigue, stress, and witchcraft. Depression and chronic stress need to be addressed through prayer, counseling, and medical intervention if necessary. Fatigue is often a symptom of imbalance in lifestyle and schedules. We are called to healthy balance in lifestyle, time for recreation, and the ability to say "no" to some ministry or service opportunities.

B) The attack of witchcraft to cause confusion in the mind and immune system can be subtle, but with experience the prayer minister can discern when this is happening. The person may have had past involvement with the occult or freemasonry, or in their family, previous generations may have been involved.

C. In their course called Elijah House Ministry, the Sandfords talk in one section about awakening the slumbering spirit of a person. It involves speaking and ministering directly to the spirit of a person, and calling them awake to their destiny, to their identity as sons and daughters of God, and to the promises of God.

Notes

Chapter 5: A Five Step Prayer Model

The Commission

Healing was Central to the Ministry of Jesus

Healing the sick was an integral part of the ministry of Jesus. In most places where the gospel speaks generally about His ministry, healing is mentioned. Matthew 4:23 is one example:

Matthew 4:23

Now Jesus went about all Galilee, teaching in their synagogues, preaching the gospel of the kingdom, and healing all kinds of sickness and all kinds of disease among the people.

Healing was also part of Jesus' assignment to the twelve disciples:

Matthew 10:1, 5, 7-8

And when He had called His twelve disciples to Him, He gave them power over unclean spirits, to cast them out, and to heal all kinds of sickness and all kinds of disease… These twelve Jesus sent out and commanded them, saying, "… as you go, preach, saying, 'The kingdom of heaven is at hand.' Heal the sick, cleanse the lepers, raise the dead, cast out demons. Freely you have received, freely give."

---

and to the seventy:

Luke 10:1-2, 9

After these things the Lord appointed seventy others also, and sent them two by two before His face into every city and place where He Himself was about to go. Then He said to them, "…And heal the sick who are there, and say to them, 'The kingdom of God has come near to you."

Healing is part of the great commission assigned now to all believers:

Mark 16:15-18

And He said to them, "Go into all the world and preach the gospel to every creature. He who believes and is baptized will be saved; but he who does not believe will be condemned. And these signs will follow those who believe: In My name they will cast out demons; they will speak with new tongues; they will take up serpents; and if they drink anything deadly, it will by no means hurt them; they will lay hands on the sick, and they will recover."

Therefore, ministering in the name of Jesus to the sick, with laying on of hands, is for "those who believe". Of course this includes every member of the body of Christ!

Your Preparation

Preparation for ministry for the healing of others is very important.

Try to be a clean, clear channel for God to use!

Be "prayed up"! Pray a lot in tongues both before and during ministry time. If you don't pray in tongues, ask God fervently and specifically to be with you and to help you. He is the healer. If He doesn't come, the person you pray for won't get healed.

Take a moment to ask the Holy Spirit if there is anyone you need to forgive. If there is, forgive him or her at once from your heart. See Matthew 6:14-15.

Ask the Holy Spirit to show you any unconfessed sin in your life. If He does, repent sincerely at once and ask God's forgiveness for it. See Luke 13:2-5.

Ask God to give you His love for each person you pray for. A loving ministry will impact the sick person for good, whether or not his body is healed. He may not really know that God loves him. Your ministry may be his first experience of God's love.

Be aware that physical healing may take different routes. It may be instantaneous. It may come gradually in stages as you pray. It may come after repeated times of ministry. Or it may not come at all. God is sovereign. He heals when, how and whom He chooses in His own wisdom. Do not be put off if God does not heal someone you minister to. Our job is to pray. God is responsible for what does or does not happen.

Do not worry if the sick person does not seem to have faith for his healing. Faith helps. But God sometimes heals sick people who don't believe He can or will heal them. (And sometimes when the one who prays does not have much faith either!)

Be flexible. There is no universal rule about how to pray that will apply to all cases. There is nothing special in particular words. The Holy Spirit is the only sure guide. He may lead you differently from time to time. Practice listening to Him and following His leading.

The Holy Spirit may ask you to pray for something the person has not mentioned to you. In that case, include it in your prayer. But be clear, careful and tactful!

Review the Ministry Team Protocol and the Prayer Guidelines at the front of this Manual.

A Five-Step Model for Healing

There are different ways of praying for the sick. The following Five-Step model is not the only one. If you have found one that is effective for you, use it in your own personal ministry.

This Five-Step model is used by Randy Clark and ministry teams at Global Awakening crusades and events. It is quiet, loving and effective. It can be used by anyone.

The five steps are:

1. **The Interview**

2. **Prayer Selection**

3. **Prayer Ministry**

4. **Stop and Re-interview**

5. **Post-prayer Suggestions**

Step One: The Interview

Briefly interview the person requesting prayer. Be attentive and gentle. A loving attitude on your part will do much to reassure the person that he is in good hands. Ask him or her what the physical need is, but do not go into lengthy detail. For example:

"What is your name?" (*A question or two to put the person at ease.*)

"What would you like prayer for?"

"How long have you had this condition?"

"Do you know what the cause is?"

"Have you seen a doctor?"... "What does he say is the matter?"

"Do you remember what was happening in your life when this condition started?"

"Did anything traumatic happen to you about the time your condition began, or within a few months prior to it starting?"

[You may need to explain to the prayee why you are asking these last two questions.]

This is often sufficient for the initial interview. You may now know the nature and cause of the condition. In some cases you won't know and must ask additional questions, or simply ask the Holy Spirit for His leading. If His leading isn't clear to you, you must make an educated guess as to the nature and cause of the condition.

For example:

Perhaps there was an accident, which would usually suggest a natural cause. (But, he may need to forgive the person who caused the accident. This could mean himself, if he caused it.)

Perhaps he was born with the condition, which would often suggest a natural cause, or possibly a generational curse.

The condition may be partly or totally caused by emotional stress. Perhaps the person has had headaches ever since he lost a job. Maybe his back has hurt ever since someone cheated him. Or perhaps cancer was discovered a few months after a divorce, or after the death of a parent or child.

The cause might be spiritual. Perhaps the person has had nightmares since an occult experience he had. Maye his condition is the result of a habitual sin, or perhaps the effect of a curse of some kind.

As noted above, if the cause is not known, ask the Holy Spirit for His leading as to the nature and possible cause of the condition. However, during your prayer for healing you may want to consider possible other causes of the condition than the one you first considered, or you may want to go back to the interview stage and ask further questions. (See the comments under Step Four on re-interviewing the person.)

Step Two: Prayer Selection

In the prayer selection, one must decide on the appropriate type of prayer ministry.

Types of prayer ministry:

Petition: A request to heal, addressed to God, to Jesus, or to the Holy Spirit.

"Father, in the name of Jesus I ask you to restore sight to this eye."

"Father, I pray in Jesus' name, come and straighten this spine."

"Father, release Your power to heal, in Jim's body, in the name of Jesus."

"Come, Holy Spirit. Release your power. Touch Jim's back, in Jesus' name."

Command: A command addressed to a condition of the body, or to a part of the body, or to a troubling spirit such as a spirit of pain, or infirmity, or of affliction.

"In the name of Jesus, I command this tumor to shrivel up and dissolve."

"In the name of Jesus, spine, be straight! Be healed!"

"In Jesus' name, I command every afflicting spirit; get out of Jim's body."

"In the name of Jesus, I command all pain and swelling to leave this ankle."

A command is appropriate:

As your initial step, unless you are led otherwise by the Holy Spirit.

When there has been a word of knowledge for healing or some other indication that God wants to heal the person at this time.

When petition prayers have been tried and progress has stopped.

When casting out an afflicting spirit or any other spirit.

When a curse or vow is broken.

Whenever you are so led by the Holy Spirit.

As preliminaries to praying for healing.

Step Three: Prayer Ministry

First, audibly ask the Holy Spirit to come. You can say simply, "Come, Holy Spirit!" Or, "Come, Holy Spirit, with Your healing power." Or you may prefer a longer prayer. Then wait on Him for a minute or two.

Tell the person receiving ministry that you will be quiet for a minute or two, so that he doesn't become confused about what is going on.

An Attitude of Receiving

Ask the person not to pray while you are praying for him. Here again, be gentle and loving. Say something like: "I know this means a lot to you, and you have probably prayed a lot about your condition. But for now I need you to focus on your body. I want you to just relax and to let me know if anything begins to happen in your body, like heat, tingling, electricity, a change in the amount or location of the pain, etc. If you are praying in English, or in tongues or thanking Jesus, or saying 'Yes, Yes!', it is harder for you to focus on your body. It is harder for you to receive healing."

Sometimes a person may find it very hard not to pray. Don't be hung up on this. Pray for him anyway.

If the presence of the Holy Spirit becomes evident, as by the person feeling heat or tingling or some other manifestation, continue waiting on Him until He finishes what He wishes to do at that time. When the manifestation has ebbed, check to see if healing is complete. If it is not complete, continue your ministry.

Remember: <u>always</u> pray or command in the name of Jesus!

Mark 16:17-18

In my name … they will lay hands on the sick, and they will recover.

Colossians 3:17

And whatever you do in word or deed, do all in the name of the Lord Jesus, giving thanks to God the Father through Him.

You cannot use the name of Jesus too much! The power is in His name. Some who have anointed healing ministries sometimes simply repeat "In the name of Jesus", over and over as their prayer for healing.

Thank God for whatever He does. You cannot thank God too much!

When you minister healing, seek to deal with the cause of the condition if you know the cause, as well as with the symptoms. For example:

"Father, in Jesus' name I ask you to heal the cones and rods in the retina of this eye. Father, in the name of Jesus, cause the scar tissue to dissolve and leave this eye. Oh God, restore the sight in this

eye, in the name of Jesus."

"In the name of Jesus, I command this ruptured disc to be healed and filled with fluid, and every pinched nerve to be released and soothed. In the name of Jesus, I command the pain to leave Joe's back."

"In the name of Jesus, dear God, I ask You to heal this pancreas. Father, in the name of Jesus I ask You to touch this pancreas with your healing power and cause it to function normally. Cause it to produce insulin as needed and cause all diabetes to be cured and complete health restored. Release Your healing in the name of Jesus."

"In the name of Jesus, I command every afflicting spirit and every spirit of infirmity, leave Joe's body, now!"

"In Jesus' name I command all stiffness to leave this joint, all pain to leave and all swelling to subside. I command all calcium deposits and all scar tissue to dissolve in Jesus' name."

"In Jesus' name, I command all chemical imbalances in Joe's body to be healed.

I command every organ furnishing chemicals or other signals to his organs to function normally in Jesus' name."

Forgiveness of Another's Wrong Conduct

If it appears that someone else caused the condition or that someone wronged the person about the time the condition started, find out if the sick person has forgiven the other. If not, forgiveness should precede your prayer for healing. Unforgiveness can be a major obstacle to healing.

If you think forgiveness is called for, ask the sick person to forgive the other, even if the sick person is not aware of any resentment toward that person.

Examples:

A woman has had arthritis in her spine for five years, ever since her husband ran off with another woman. Has she forgiven her husband and the woman? Jesus said we must forgive, not we ought to. Emotional stress can cause illness, pre-vent healing. Sometimes one can be angry at God and must forgive Him.

A pastor has had back pain for ten years. Ten years ago there was a split in his church and some of his closest friends turned against him. Has he forgiven the ringleaders of the split, his former friends, and all others involved?

(Note: Sometimes a person is healed before you even begin to pray for healing, just by forgiving the person who caused the hurt, or just by repenting and asking God's forgiveness for his own sin of resentment and anger. The pastor noted above was healed by forgiving without any prayer for healing.)

Repentance for One's Own Wrong Conduct and Asking Forgiveness for It

If it appears that the condition was brought on by sin, very gently inquire if the person agrees that this might be so. If he does, encourage him to repent and ask God's forgiveness. This should precede your prayer for healing. Sin that is not repented for can impede healing. Anger can contribute to back pain and some depressions. AIDS may result from a wrong lifestyle. Lung cancer might have been caused by smoking.

But, be tender. Ask if perhaps the condition could be related to his lifestyle. Perhaps say, "I wonder if this condition could be related to things you have done in the past." Never accuse the person confrontationally of causing his condition by his sin. It is seldom helpful and you may be wrong.

A caution: If this leading is of the Holy Spirit, the Holy Spirit will usually indicate the specific sin which is the problem, not sin in general. General accusations of sin are often destructive and probably are from the enemy.

A person may need to forgive himself. He may have caused his own injury or sickness. This may seem unnecessary but it sometimes releases healing.

Some Practical Suggestions on How to Minister

If changes in the seeker's condition can be readily determined, it is appropriate and often helpful to pray short prayers or give brief commands interspersed with re-interviewing at frequent intervals to see if progress is being made.

"What has happened to the pain now?"

"See if you can read the sign now."

"Do you still feel heat in your stomach?"

"Try moving your knee now."

(A person may be partly or completely healed without feeling anything. He may not realize that healing has taken place until he uses the affected part. If he does something he could not do before or that caused pain before, he can see if the prayer thus far has made a difference.)

When a prayer or command results in a partial healing, continue to use it until you find that it no longer produces further healing.

Two examples of short prayers with frequent interviews, in actual situations, are set out in Examples 1 and 2 at the end of this section.

Note that many of the prayers or commands for healing set out in scripture are very short.

"I am willing. Be cleansed." (Mark 1:41)

"Little girl, I say to you 'Arise.'" (Mark 5:41)

"God, be merciful to me, a sinner!" (Luke 18:13)

"Please heal her, O God, I pray!" (Num. 12:13)

"In the name of Jesus Christ of Nazareth, rise up and walk!" (Acts 3:6)

"Jesus the Christ heals you. Arise and make your bed." (Acts 9:34)

"Brother Saul, the Lord Jesus, who appeared to you on the road as you came, has sent me that you may receive your sight and be filled with the Holy Spirit." (Acts 9:17)

If a long prayer is followed by partial healing, it is hard to know what part of the prayer or command was effective. Then if it is to be repeated, the entire prayer may have to be repeated.

However, short prayers are not always called for. Where progress cannot readily be determined, such as with diabetes, frequent interviewing is not useful unless there are manifestations which help you to know what is going on. For example, if there is heat and the heat intensifies with certain prayers, then short prayers with frequent interviews may be appropriate.

Even if short prayers are appropriate, healing may not come after the short prayers. But healing will sometimes come after an extended time of prayer or after many prayers or after several times of praying.

Be Persistent

If you try one kind of prayer or command and get results but not complete healing, continue. Explain why you are continuing to the person receiving prayer or he may wonder about the repetition. Be persistent!

If you try one kind of prayer or command and get no result after a few times, try another kind! Be persistent!

Sometimes a person expects you to pray only once for his condition and then stop. So if he is not healed promptly, he may expect you to stop praying and he may start to leave. Encourage him to stay and let you pray more. Continue praying as long as God seems to be making any further change in his condition or as long as you are given different ways to pray for him. Be persistent!

If healing has partially come and then seems to stop, wait a bit. Continue praying for a time to see whether another wave of healing will come. Be persistent!

Your Manner

You need not necessarily pray aloud all the time. If you wish, tell the person that you may pray silently at times. As long as you have your hand on his arm you are praying, even if not aloud.   And do pray silently. Listen to the Holy Spirit. He may give you some guidance you would otherwise miss.

It is often very helpful to pray with your eyes open, and observe the person you are praying for. Look for signs that God is at work in his body: fluttering eyelids, trembling, perspiration. If you see something happening or if the person reports a change in the pain or increased sight or other progress, thank God for what He is doing and bless it. Continue to pray in the manner that led to the progress.

If you are not accustomed to praying with your eyes open, this will require practice! However, it is worth the practice as it sometimes helps you see what God is doing.

Use your normal tone of voice. Shouting or praying loudly in tongues will not increase your effectiveness.

Don't preach, don't give advice and don't prophesy.

Step Four: Stop and Re-Interview

If after a time you are making no progress, consider interviewing the person further.

Possible questions might be:

> *"Would you try again to remember whether anything significant happened within six months or so of the beginning of this condition?"* (Some event may require forgiveness that the person may have forgotten or may have been unwilling to disclose.)

> *"Do any other members of your family have this condition?"* (If so, perhaps there is a generational spirit affecting several members of the family.)

> *"Do you have a strong fear of anything?"* (Fear can be a cause of many physical and spiritual problems, and it sometimes interferes with healing.)

> *"Is anyone in your family a member of the Freemasons or Eastern Star?"* (Association with Masonic or other occult organizations is particularly likely to impede healing.)

> *"Has anyone ever cursed you or your family that you know of?"*

> *"Have you had other accidents?"* (If the person is accident-prone, consider whether he is under a curse.)

> *"Have you ever participated in any kind of occult game or practice?"*

Consider whether a Wrong Spirit may be Present

If the person reports that the pain has moved or has increased, it signals the likely presence of an afflicting spirit. Simply command the afflicting spirit to leave in the name of Jesus. You might pray with more intensity, but not louder. "In the name of Jesus, I break the power of this afflicting spirit and command it to leave Joe's body!" Or an equivalent prayer.

If the condition has existed a long time or if it is a condition that resists medical treatment such as cancer, diabetes, Parkinson's, AIDS, etc. Consider that there is likely to be a spirit causing the condition or resisting healing and command it to leave. "In the name of Jesus, I command any spirit of arthritis to leave this woman!"

(When expelling a spirit of infirmity or an afflicting spirit or a spirit of a particular condition, a simple prayer may be enough. But see section on "Deliverance" for help in cases where expelling a spirit seems more difficult.)

Inner Healing

Very often a person who requests prayer for a physical problem is also in need of emotional healing from hurts and wounds suffered as a result of trauma, physical or emotional abuse, perceived or real rejection, disappointments, fears, perceived or real inadequacies, and so on. These hurts and wounds may have accumulated over a long period of years.

Sometimes the physical healing of such a person cannot be fully realized unless and until his inner wounds and hurts have been healed or a process of healing begun.

Sometimes, even if a person seems to receive physical healing it may be apparent that emotional healing is also needed.

Sometimes the person thinks his problem is physical, or sometimes you or he may think he needs deliverance. However, what he really needs is inner healing.

In these cases, you should by all means take time to pray for the person's inner healing. Follow the leading of the Holy Spirit. Pray for the healing of hurts that have become apparent in your conversation with the sick person. If you are so led, inquire gently about the causes of the inner hurts. If circumstances permit, take time to understand the situations at least in general. If time is limited, consider scheduling another session with the sick person.

Pray for the healing of each specific hurt just as you would for each specific physical ailment.[1] It is appropriate to inquire from time to time whether the Holy Spirit has put additional specific needs on the person's mind that you might pray for.

Allow the prayee to weep. Encourage it if he begins to cry. Let God love, comfort and console the person through you. When emotions are very strong, it is often helpful to ask Jesus to speak to the person or to show him how Jesus sees his situation. You may know other effective methods of praying for inner healing.

Ministry to a Person Who is Under Medical Care

You will have occasion to minister to people who are consulting with a counselor or psychiatrist. This probably is not a problem if your ministry is for a physical ailment such as a broken limb or back pain. However, if healing for emotional problems is indicated, you should ask the prayee to get the approval of his doctor or counselor for his seeking prayer. This is especially important if the prayee is under medication.

Sometimes a person under medication, such as for diabetes, asthma, arthritis, heart disease, etc., believes he has been healed when you pray for him. He may think he can discontinue his medication. You must instruct him to continue his medication after your ministry to him; even if he believes and even if you believe he has been healed. He must return to his doctor and let the doctor change his medication if the doctor considers it appropriate to do so.

Ministry to a Person with Multiple Problems

As a general rule, it is better to finish praying for one condition before starting to pray for another unless the Holy Spirit directs you differently. Flitting from one problem to another is distracting. The person's faith will be built up for successive problems if one healing is completed.

---

[1] *Francis McNutt says specificity is particularly important in prayer for inner healing.*

The sick person may ask you to pray for a second problem as soon as you finish your first prayer for one condition. He may not understand that you will pray further for the first condition. Tell him gently that you will pray for the second condition. But first you wish to finish praying for the first condition.

Follow the leading of the Holy Spirit! If you are praying for a person's sinus infection and his bad foot begins to tingle, stop praying for the sinus condition and pray for the foot. Bless what God is doing and pray in cooperation with what He is doing. Go back to the sinus only when you have finished praying for the foot or when the sinus begins to manifest the presence of God at work there.

Other

Ask the Holy Spirit for His leading and expect to receive it.

Don't cause guilt in the person you are ministering to. Don't make him feel guilty if he does not get healed. Don't tell him it is his fault even if you think it is!

If you think you may have made a mistake don't fret over it. The Holy Spirit is bigger than your mistakes!

If possible, always use a catcher. A person may fall even though you are praying only for his physical healing. If you don't have a catcher, have the prayee sit down or stand against a wall so that he cannot fall or have the person stand in front of a chair so that if he becomes weak he can settle into the chair.

If the prayee falls, pray for him a few moments longer and then see if he has been healed ("How is the pain now?" "Try moving your neck now." etc.). Ask if he senses that the Holy Spirit is still touching him. If he senses that God is still at work in him, pray further for him. If nothing seems to be happening, ask the Holy Spirit whether you are through praying for him and continue as long as the Holy Spirit wants you to.

When to Stop Praying

Stop praying when:

> The person is completely healed.
>
> The person wants you to stop. He may be tired or simply feel you should stop.
>
> The Holy Spirit tells you it is time to stop.
>
> You are not given any other way to pray and you are not gaining ground.

Step Five: Post-Prayer Suggestions

After praying, consider the following:

Encourage the prayee's walk with the Lord.

You might share a scripture verse. For some people, scriptural passages are extremely meaningful and encouraging.

If a condition resulted from occult experiences or habitual sin, suggest tactfully that a change in lifestyle may well be needed to avoid a recurrence of his condition.

If he is not healed or not completely healed, don't accuse him of lack of faith for healing or of sin in his life as the cause.

Encourage the person to get prayer from others if there is little or no evidence of healing, or if his healing has not been completed. Encourage him to come back again for more prayer after the next meeting, etc. Sometimes healing is progressive and sometimes it occurs only after a number of prayers for healing have been made.

Tell the prayee not to be surprised if he experiences a spiritual attack after a healing. Help him to be prepared to resist it. If a symptom starts to recur, he can command it to leave in Jesus' name. If a bad habit is involved, he may be tempted for a short time to re-commence the habit. If he does yield, quick repentance is needed and asking God's help to overcome.

Love! Love! Love!

As a minister of healing, do everything in love.

An Observation

1 Corinthians 16:14

Let all that you do be done with love.

1 Corinthians 13:4 RSV

Love is patient... kind... not jealous... not arrogant or rude.

1 Corinthians 13:4-5 Phillips

Love is not anxious to impress... not touchy.

If you pray for more people, you will see more people healed!

Example 1: Short Prayers on Back Pain

Back Pain

Example of an interview and prayer exchange between a pray-er (**P**) and a person with severe back pain (**A**). This illustrates the use of short prayers interspersed with interviews. It is a closely approximate account of an actual event.

The Situation

A comes to **P** with a friend for help with a bad back. **A**'s back hurts so much that she has to ease herself down into a chair when she sits down and has to struggle painfully to stand up again.

The Preliminary Steps

P: "Where does your back hurt?"

A: (Pointing.) "All across this part of my back."

P: "When did your back start hurting?"

A: "About three months ago."

P: "Do you know what caused it?"

A: "I hurt my back moving some furniture."

P: "Have you seen a doctor about this?"

A: "A chiropractor. He treats me for a vertebra that has slipped out of place."

P: "Has he helped you?"

A: "Yes, each time I see him. But the pain comes back and it's getting worse."

P: "Did you need help moving the furniture?"

A: (Bitterly) "I asked my husband to help me move it but he wouldn't. He never helps me with anything around the house."

P: "Do you need to forgive him?"

A: "I suppose so."

P leads **A** in a prayer of forgiveness for her husband for not helping to move the furniture, releasing him to God, undertaking not to try to change him herself, and blessing him.

Note: At this point **P** could have led **A** in a prayer forgiving her husband for <u>all</u> the hurts he has caused her. This should be done at some point. If it not done now, **P** should suggest that **A** do this soon.

P: "Now let's take a reading on your back. Try moving it. How is the pain now?" **A** moves her back.

A: (Surprised.) "Well, it's a lot better!"

P: "Is the pain completely gone?"

Note: anger is a frequent cause of or contributor to back pain. Sometimes a person is completely healed just in the act of forgiving the one who has caused the pain.

A: "No, but it's a lot less."

P: "Well, now let's pray for it. Let me check your legs first."

The Ministry

P checks **A**'s legs and finds that one is a little shorter than the other. **P** prays for the short leg to lengthen, which it does. **P** asks **A** to stand up and see if the pain has changed in her back.

A: "Well, it's still better. But I get a twinge right here." (A touches her back.)

P: Puts his hand on the spot that hurts. "*In the name of Jesus, I command all pain to leave A's back.* Now try your back again."

A: "It's good. Very good."

P: "Is the pain all gone?"

A: "I would say just about all. It's some stiff and sore."

P: (Puts his hand on **A**'s back.) "*In the name of Jesus, I command every spirit of pain or soreness or stiffness to get out of A's back.* Now let's check it again."

In this case, the pain was now completely gone and the prayer ended. **P** asks **A** to thank Jesus for healing her.

Notes

If the pain had not completely gone, **P** might have given one or more of the following commands until the pain left completely, or until there was no more progress.

"that all the vertebrae in **A**'s back line up properly, one squarely on top of the other."

"that all the discs in **A**'s back take their proper size and shape and location."

"that every pinched nerve be released, and every damaged nerve be healed."

"that all extra calcium deposits or growths in **A**'s back dissolve and be gone."

Also, if **A** had a pain running down one of her legs, it is likely to be from a pinched or damaged sciatic nerve. If such a pain develops at the time that **P** is praying for **A**'s back, it may be caused by a spirit of sciatica. **P** could pray as follows, as appropriate:

"In the name of Jesus, I command **A**'s sciatic nerve to be healed."

or,

"In the name of Jesus, I command the spirit of sciatica to get out of **A**'s body."

(After praying in this way, **P** would check for change in the pain.)

In the real case, **P** then asked **A** to pray a prayer of thanksgiving and asking the Holy Spirit to come and fill **A** up.

In this case, **A** was encouraged to walk continually in forgiveness of her husband. Her back was still well after about 8 months. So it appears that the healing was permanent.

This example is not intended as a comment on other types of prayer for healing. God uses all types of prayers. As one example, God sometimes heals with the simple prayer, "God, please heal Sally." Or, "Sally's back be healed, in the name of Jesus!" See Moses' prayer for Miriam: *"Please heal her, O God, I pray!"* (Numbers 12:13.)

Similarly, it is not intended as a comment on longer prayer times. There are some situations that call for unhurried longer prayer times. Also, even if short prayers are appropriate in a given situation, if healing does not come soon longer prayer times may result in healing.

The point of the above example is simply that praying short prayers with frequent interviews is often an effective way to pray and can result in healing within a rather short time frame.

Example 2:

Short Prayers on Person with Injury to Chest and Arm Muscles, and Inability to Lift Arm

[An example of exchanges between a person with pain, weakness in some of his left arm and chest muscles, inability to raise his left arm to shoulder height (**A**) and the person praying for him (**P**). This also was an actual situation with a successful conclusion.]

The Interview

P: (After **A** has explained his condition.) "How did this all happen? Did you have an accident?"

A: "I'm a courier. I was delivering a package for a messenger service and ran into a thick glass door that I thought was open. I hit my shoulder and bent my arm. I was really stupid. It was my fault. I was partly drunk. Now I can't lift a heavy package or ride a bicycle. I can't lift my arm above this high (demonstrating). So, I can't get any kind of a job that requires much use of my arm."

P: "When did this happen?"

A: "About seven years ago."

P: "Have you forgiven yourself for being drunk and for running into the door?"

A: "No, it hasn't occurred to me that I need to forgive myself."

The Ministry

P: "Well, let's do it anyway."

P leads **A** in a prayer of repentance for taking alcohol into his body and asking God's forgiveness, and of repentance for being partly drunk, for being careless as a courier, asking God's forgiveness and forgiving himself for the whole incident.

P: "Now check your chest muscles and see how they are. See how high you can raise your arm."

A: "The pain in my arm is nearly gone! My chest still hurts. I think I can lift my arm higher." A tries lifting his arm. He can lift it a bit higher, but not much.

P: "All right. That's good! Now let's pray for your healing. First, we'll ask the Holy Spirit to come. We'll all just be quiet for a minute or two. You don't have to pray. Just relax and let the Holy Spirit do whatever He would like to do at this time. *Holy Spirit, please come with Your healing power.*"

Everyone is quiet for a minute or so. **A** feels heat in his chest. **P** thanks God for what He is doing. When the heat subsides, **A** still has pain in his chest, slight pain in his arm and cannot raise his arm higher than the last time he tried.

P: "Let's pray for the pain in your chest muscles." **P** lays his hand lightly on **A**'s chest. "*In the name of Jesus, I command **A**'s chest muscles to be healed. I command all bruising to leave and the effect of all the past bruising to be healed.* Now check your chest and see if the pain has changed either for the worse or the better."

A: "The pain in my chest is much less. It's almost gone now too."

P: (Repeating) "Well, that prayer seemed to make some progress, we'll pray that one again. *In the name of Jesus, I command **A**'s chest muscles to be healed. I command all bruising to leave and the effect of all the past bruising to be healed, in Jesus' name!* Now check again to see if anything further has happened to the pain."

A: "The pain in my chest is completely gone!"

P: "Try pushing on my hand and see if your arm or chest hurts."

A pushes on **P**'s hand and says the arm and the chest do not hurt. **P** says to push harder. **A** pushes very hard on **P**'s hand but has no pain.

P: "Well, thank Jesus for healing your arm and chest! You know He is the healer."

A: "Yes, I will!"

P: "Let's do it right now."

A: "Thank you Jesus for healing my arm and chest."

P: "I think you will find the strength has returned to your arm. However, if it isn't completely healed, come back and get prayer for it again another time."

A: "Thanks, I will!"

P: "Now let's pray for your arm movement." **P** lays his hand on **A**'s shoulder. *"In the name of Jesus, I command **A**'s arm to be healed. In Jesus' name, I command all the muscles and ligaments in his arm to function normally so that he can raise his arm normally.* Now try raising your arm."

A tries to raise his arm with somewhat more success but not a lot more. **P** repeats his prayer until improvement stops.

P: "I'm going to raise your arm with my hand but I don't want to hurt you. You tell me at once if this hurts."

P raises **A**'s arm a bit. "Does that hurt?" **A** says it doesn't hurt, so **P** raises the arm farther. "Does this hurt?" **P** repeats this once more and **A** says the arm hurts a little. **P** holds the arm up and commands the pain to leave.

P: "Okay. Now you see if you can raise your arm that much."

A: "Well, I can't raise it as far as you did, but much more than I could before."

P repeats lifting **A**'s arm until there is slight pain and commanding the pain to leave. **A** gains a little more lift when trying to raise his arm.

P: "Just in case there is one present I'm going to cast out any spirit of infirmity in your arm. *In the name of Jesus, I command any spirit of infirmity in **A** or in his arm to get out of him now! In the name of Jesus, I command any afflicting spirit to get out of him now! Your assignments are over*! Now, try your arm again."

A: "This is amazing! I can't raise it all the way, but almost. And it doesn't hurt at all."

P prayed three or four more times for healing of the muscles and ligaments in **A**'s shoulder. He lifted **A**'s arm until **A** felt discomfort and then commanded the muscles and nerves to be healed and the pain to leave. Eventually, **A** had complete move-ment of his left arm without pain. It seemed that he was com-pletely healed. **P** had **A** thank Jesus for healing him and then prayed for filling with the Holy Spirit and a general prayer of blessing over **A**.

Notes

After eight or nine months, **A**'s arm still had full movement and its strength had returned. It seems that his healing was permanent.

Chapter 6: A Biblical Theology for Healing

Lesson Goals

1) To gain a solid Biblical basis for the ministry of healing as it relates to:
   A) The nature of God
   B) Messianic prophecy
   C) The covenant, the atonement, and the kingdom of God
   D) The scope of healing
2) To understand the commission of healing to all believers.
3) To understand the model of humility, the mystery, and the motivation of healing as it relates to our moving in healing.
4) To receive faith for healing as the message is taught and to respond to the anointing of God.
5) For people to be healed during the message.

Introduction

In this session we make a brief journey through key scriptures on the Biblical Basis of Healing. It is important in the ministry of healing to have a rock-solid foundation as to the Father's will to heal. In this way, no matter what we are faced with, we can move forward with full confidence that the Father desires to *RELEASE HEALING* through the *NAME OF JESUS,* and in the *POWER* and *ANOINTING* of the Holy Spirit.

A WORD OF PREPARATION FROM RANDY:

Today, while I am preaching the Word of God, God will heal people as they listen to the Word of God. *I WANT YOU EXPECTING TO RECEIVE!*

WHAT I WANT YOU TO DO
When you __FEEL__ the anointing, STAND to your feet and REMAIN standing until I SEE you and say, "I bless you in the name or Jesus." Then, you may be seated.

Key Insights

Healing is inclusive of the ministry of deliverance and raising the dead.

I) Healing is one of the seven aspects of God's self-revelation.

Exodus 15:26b

[26]I will not bring on you any of the diseases I brought on the Egyptians, for I am the LORD, who heals you.

Acts 10:38

[38]How God anointed Jesus of Nazareth with the Holy Spirit and power, and how he went around doing good and healing all who were under the power of the devil, because God was with him.

1 John 3:8b

[8]The reason the Son of God appeared was to destroy the devil's work.

John 14-16 - Read for yourself these awesome promises made to us by Jesus.

II) The Messiah was to be recognized by a healing and deliverance ministry.

Luke 7:20-23

[20]When the men came to Jesus, they said, "John the Baptist sent us to you to ask, 'Are you the one who was to come, or should we expect someone else?' " [21]At that very time Jesus cured many who had diseases, sicknesses and evil spirits, and gave sight to many who were blind. [22]So he replied to the messengers, "Go back and report to John what you have seen and heard: The blind receive sight, the lame walk, those who have leprosy are cured, the deaf hear, the dead are raised, and the good news is preached to the poor. [23]Blessed is the man who does not fall away on account of me."

Fulfilling Isaiah 35:5-6

[5]Then will the eyes of the blind be opened and the ears of the deaf unstopped. [6]Then will the lame leap like a deer, and the mute tongue shout for joy. Water will gush forth in the wilderness and streams in the desert.

Luke 4:18-19

[18]"The Spirit of the Lord is on me, because he has anointed me to preach good news to the poor. He has sent me to proclaim freedom for the prisoners and recovery of sight for the blind, to release the oppressed, [19]to proclaim the year of the Lord's favor."

Fulfilling Isaiah 61:1-2

[1]The Spirit of the Sovereign LORD is on me, because the LORD has anointed me to preach good news to the poor. He has sent me to bind up the brokenhearted, proclaim freedom for the captives and release from darkness for the prisoners, [2]to proclaim the year of the LORD's favor and the day of vengeance of our God, to comfort all who mourn

III) The 12 Disciples were commissioned to heal and deliver the demonized and raise the dead.

Matthew 10:1, 7-8

[1]He called his twelve disciples to him and gave them authority to drive out evil spirits and to heal every disease and sickness…[7]As you go, preach this message: "The kingdom of heaven is near." [8]Heal the sick, raise the dead, cleanse those who have leprosy, drive out demons. Freely you have received, freely give.

Mark 6:7

[7]Calling the Twelve to him, he sent them out two by two and gave them authority over evil spirits.

Mark 6:12-13

[12]They went out and preached that people should repent. [13]They drove out many demons and anointed many sick people with oil and healed them.

Luke 9:1-2

[1]When Jesus had called the Twelve together, he gave them power and authority to drive out all demons and to cure diseases, [2]and he sent them out to preach the kingdom of God and to heal the sick.

Luke 9:6

[6]So they set out and went from village to village, preaching the gospel and healing people everywhere.

IV) A larger group of disciples (70) were commissioned to heal and deliver the demonized.

Luke 10:1, 9, 17-24

[1]After this the Lord appointed seventy-two others and sent them two by two ahead of him to every town and place where he was about to go…[9]Heal the sick who are there and tell them, "The kingdom of God is near you."…[17]The seventy-two returned with joy and said, "Lord, even the demons submit to us in your name." [18]He replied, "I saw Satan fall like lightning from heaven. [19]I have given you authority to trample on snakes and scorpions and to overcome all the power of the enemy; nothing will harm you. [20]However, do not rejoice that the spirits submit to you, but rejoice that your names are written in heaven." [21]At that time Jesus, full of joy through the Holy Spirit, said, "I praise you, Father, Lord of heaven and earth, because you have hidden these things from the wise and learned, and revealed them to little children. Yes, Father, for this was your good pleasure. [22]"All things have been committed to me by my Father. No one knows who the Son is except the Father, and no one knows who the Father is except the Son and those to whom the Son chooses to reveal him." [23]Then he turned to his disciples and said privately, "Blessed are the eyes that see what you see. [24]For I tell you that many prophets and kings wanted to see what you see but did not see it, and to hear what you hear but did not hear it."

V) Every Christian is to be trained to heal the sick and deliver those who are demonized.

A) This is the primary responsibility of Apostles, Prophets, Evangelists, Pastors, and Teachers.

Matthew 28:18-20

[18]Then Jesus came to them and said, "All authority in heaven and on earth has been given to me. [19]Therefore go and make disciples of all nations, baptizing them in the name of the Father and of the Son and of the Holy Spirit, [20]and teaching them to obey everything I have commanded you. And surely I am with you always, to the very end of the age."

Ephesians 4:11-13

[11]It was he who gave some to be apostles, some to be prophets, some to be evangelists, and some to be pastors and teachers, [12]to prepare God's people for works of service, so that the body of Christ may be built up [13]until we all reach unity in the faith and in the knowledge of the Son of God and become mature, attaining to the whole measure of the fullness of Christ.

B) Not all will have the ministry of healing, deliverance, raising the dead. Neither will all be in the office of a healer or worker of miracles. But all can minister healing and deliverance out of their role, just not as often nor as powerfully as those who have the gifts or are in the office.

1 Corinthians 12:28-31

[28]And in the church God has appointed first of all apostles, second prophets, third teachers, then workers of miracles, also those having gifts of healing, those able to help other, those with gifts of administration, and those speaking with different kinds of tongues. [29]Are all apostles? Are all prophets? Are all teachers? Do all work miracles? [30]Do all have gifs of healing? Do all speak in tongues? Do all interpret? [31]But eagerly desire the greater gifts.

VI) Every type of disease is within the possibility of being healed. There are no diseases that are impossible to be healed.

Psalms 103:2-3

²Praise the LORD, O my soul, and forget not all his benefits- ³who forgives all your sins and heals all your diseases.

VII) The basis for healing or the basis for our prayers for healing.

A) The Covenants

(1) Exodus 34:10 – *Old Covenant*

¹⁰Then the LORD said: "I am making a covenant with you. Before all your people I will do wonders never before done in any nation in all the world. The people you live among will see how awesome is the work that I, the LORD, will do for you."

(2) Hebrews 2:3-4 – *New Covenant*

³How shall we escape if we ignore such a great salvation? This salvation, which was first announced by the Lord, was confirmed to us by those who heard him. ⁴God also testified to it by signs, wonders and various miracles, and gifts of the Holy Spirit distributed according to his will.

(3) Hebrews is the *Better Covenant* - Hebrews 7:22, 8:6

²² Because of this oath, Jesus has become the guarantee of a better covenant.

⁶ But the ministry Jesus has received is as superior to theirs as the covenant of which he is mediator is superior to the old one, and it is founded on better promises.

B) The Atonement

(1) Isaiah 53:4-5 *same verbs as* Isaiah 53:11-12

⁴Surely he **took up** our infirmities and **carried** our sorrows, yet we considered him stricken by God, smitten by him, and afflicted. ⁵But he was pierced for our transgressions, he was crushed for our iniquities; the punishment that brought us peace was upon him, and by his wounds we are healed.

¹¹After the suffering of his soul, he will see the light of life and be satisfied; by his knowledge my righteous servant will justify many, and he will bear their iniquities. ¹²Therefore I will give him a portion among the great, and he will divide the spoils with the strong, because he **poured out** his life unto death, and was numbered with the transgressors. For he **bore** the sin of many, and made intercession for the transgressors.

(2) Matthew 8:16-17

¹⁶When evening came, many who were demon-possessed were brought to him, and he drove out the spirits with a word and healed all the sick. ¹⁷This was to fulfill what was spoken through the prophet Isaiah: "He took up our infirmities and carried our diseases."

(3) 1 Peter 2:24 – *past tense*

²⁴He himself bore our sins in his body on the tree, so that we might die to sins and live for righteousness; by his wounds you have been healed.

C) The Kingdom of God – Jesus and Paul (Kingdom of Heaven – Matthew, but they mean the same thing)

(1) Luke 10:9

⁹Heal the sick who are there and tell them, "The kingdom of God is near you."

(2) Luke 17:21

²¹Nor will people say, "Here it is," or "There it is," because the kingdom of God is within you.

(3) Note again the commissioning mentioned earlier. John the Baptist, Jesus, and Paul all proclaimed the gospel of the Kingdom.

D) The Promises of God

(1) Matthew 18:19

¹⁹Again, I tell you that if two of you on earth agree about anything you ask for, it will be done for you by my Father in heaven.

(2) Matthew 21:22

²²If you believe, you will receive whatever you ask for in prayer.

(3) Mark 11:22

²² "Have faith in God," Jesus answered.

(4) John 14:13

¹³And I will do whatever you ask in my name, so that the Son may bring glory to the Father.

(5) John 15:7

⁷If you remain in me and my words remain in you, ask whatever you wish, and it will be given you.

(6) 1 John 3:22

²²And receive from him anything we ask, because we obey his commands and do what pleases him.

(7) James 5:14

¹⁴Is any one of you sick? He should call the elders of the church to pray over him and anoint him with oil in the name of the Lord.

E) The Example of the New Testament Church

(1) This ministry wasn't relegated/restricted to the 12 Apostles, or even the other apostles, as has been taught by many – especially the Cessationists.

(2) This ministry was also seen in the ministry of the Evangelist Philip who was considered by many to be one of the first deacons in the Church, as well as Stephen.

Acts 6:8

[8]Now Stephen, a man full of God's grace and power, did great wonders and miraculous signs among the people.

Acts 8:6-8

[6]When the crowds heard Philip and saw the miraculous signs he did, they all paid close attention to what he said. [7]With shrieks, evil spirits came out of many, and many paralytics and cripples were healed. [8]So there was great joy in that city.

F) Also unnamed Christians spread out by persecution to Antioch.

Acts 11:19-21

[19]Now those who had been scattered by the persecution in connection with Stephen traveled as far as Phoenicia, Cyprus and Antioch, telling the message only to Jews. [20]Some of them, however, men from Cyprus and Cyrene, went to Antioch and began to speak to Greeks also, telling them the good news about the Lord Jesus. [21]The Lord's hand was with them, *(this phrase means that God was doing supernatural things through them)* and a great number of people believed and turned to the Lord.

G) The healing ministry was part of the responsibility of the office of Elder.

James 5:14-16

[14]Is any one of you sick? He should call the elders of the church to pray over him and anoint him with oil in the name of the Lord.[15]And the prayer offered in faith will make the sick person well; the Lord will raise him up. If he has sinned, he will be forgiven. [16]Therefore confess your sins to each other and pray for each other so that you may be healed. The prayer of a righteous man is powerful and effective.

5) Implications of Scriptures teach this ministry could be experienced by the rank and file of the Christians who were not in an office.

1 Corinthians 12:9-10a

[9]To another faith by the same Spirit, to another gifts of healing by the one Spirit, [10]to another miraculous powers, to another prophecy…

Matthew 28:18-20 - The Great Commission

[18]Then Jesus came to them and said, "All authority in heaven and on earth has been given to me. [19]Therefore go and make disciples of all nations, baptizing them in the name of the Father and of the Son and of the

Holy Spirit, [20]and teaching them to obey everything I have commanded you. And surely I am with you always, to the very end of the age."

Mark 16:17,18c, 20 - Another Commissioning

[17]And these signs will accompany those who believe: in my name they will drive out demons . . . [18]they will place their hands on sick people, and they will get well… [20]Then the disciples went out and preached everywhere and the Lord worked with them and confirmed his word by the signs that accompanied it. *(Note: It doesn't say that the signs accompanied them, but that the signs accompanied it (His word)).*

VIII) The Mystery of Healing

A) There are times of greater anointing/power for healing.

(1) Examples of greater anointing for healing in the ministry of Jesus

Luke 5:17b

[17]And the power of the Lord was present for him to heal the sick.

(2) Examples of greater anointing for healing in the ministry of Paul

Acts 19:11

[11]God did extraordinary miracles through Paul, so that even handkerchiefs and aprons that had touched him were taken to the sick, and their illnesses were cured and the evil spirits left them.

B) There are times of lesser anointing/power for healing.

(1) Examples of lesser anointing in the ministry of Jesus.

Mark 6:5-6

[5]He could not do any miracles there, except lay his hands on a few sick people and heal them. [6]And he was amazed by their lack of faith.

(2) Examples of lesser anointing in the ministry of Paul.

2 Timothy 4:20b

[20]And I left Trophimus sick in Miletus.

IX) The motivation for healing

A) That the name of Jesus would be held in high honor.

Acts 19:11-17

[11]God did extraordinary miracles through Paul, [12]so that even handkerchiefs and aprons that had touched

him were taken to the sick, and their illnesses were cured and the evil spirits left them. [13] Some Jews who went around driving out evil spirits tried to invoke the name of the Lord Jesus over those who were demon-possessed. They would say, "In the name of Jesus, whom Paul preaches, I command you to come out." [14] Seven sons of Sceva, a Jewish chief priest, were doing this. [15] One day the evil spirit answered them, "Jesus I know, and I know about Paul, but who are you?" [16] Then the man who had the evil spirit jumped on them and overpowered them all. He gave them such a beating that they ran out of the house naked and bleeding. [17] When this became known to the Jews and Greeks living in Ephesus, they were all seized with fear, **and the name of the Lord Jesus was held in high honor.**

B) That Jesus and the Father would receive glory through the fruit of Christian's supernatural ministry - the "greater things."

John 14:12-14
[12]I tell you the truth, anyone who has faith in me will do what I have been doing. He will do even greater things than these, because I am going to the Father. [13]And I will do whatever you ask in my name, so that the Son may bring glory to the Father. [14]You may ask me for anything in my name, and I will do it.

John 15:7-8
[7]If you remain in me and my words remain in you, ask whatever you wish, and it will be given to you. [8]This is to my Father's glory, that you bear much fruit, showing yourselves to be my disciples.

John 16:14, 15
[14]He (the Holy Spirit) will bring glory to me by taking from what is mine and making it known to you. [15]All that belongs to the Father is mine. That is why I said the Spirit will take from what is mine and make it known to you.

X) The importance of humility and _dependence_ in the healing ministry.

(This issue of dependence is vitally important to understanding the difference between theistic healing and pantheistic healing, between Christian and pre-Christian healing, Hindu and Buddhist, New Age or Neo-Pagan.)

A) Peter, the first Teflon Christian, wouldn't let the praise of men stick to him, but directed it to Jesus.

Acts 3:12, 16
[12]When Peter saw this, he said to them: "Men of Israel, why does this surprise you? Why do you stare at us as if by our own power or godliness we had made this man walk? ... [16]By faith in the name of Jesus, this man whom you see and know was made strong. It is Jesus' name and the faith that comes through him that has given this complete healing to him, as you can all see.

B) "God resists the proud, but gives grace to the humble."

1 Peter 5:5b-6
[5]All of you, clothe yourselves with humility toward one another, because, "God opposes the proud, but gives grace to the humble." [6]Humble yourselves, therefore, under God's mighty hand, that he may lift you up

in due time.

C) This is not a false humility, but is based on our being in a dependent role for healing to occur. Unlike the New Agers, it is not "our" power but "His" power.

D) Examples of dependence

(1) Jesus

John 5:19, 30
[19]Jesus gave them this answer: "I tell you the truth, the son can do nothing by himself; he can do only what he sees his father doing, because whatever the Father does the Son also does." … [30]"By myself I can do nothing."

(2) Paul

Colossians 1:29
[29]To this end I labor, struggling with all *his energy*, which so powerfully works in me.

1 Corinthians 15:10
[10]But by the grace of God I am what I am, and his grace to me was not without effect. No, I worked harder than all of them – yet not I, but the grace of God that was with me.

Ephesians 1:18-20
[18]I pray also that the eyes of your heart may be enlightened in order that you may know the hope to which he has called you, the riches of his glorious inheritance in the saints, [19]and his incomparably great power for us who believe. That power is like the working of his mighty strength, [20]which he exerted in Christ when he raised him from the dead and seated him at his right hand in the heavenly realms.

Ephesians 3:7
[7]I became a servant of this gospel by the gift of God's grace given me through the working of his power.

Ephesians 3:14-21
[14]For this reason I kneel before the Father, [15]from whom his whole family in heaven and on earth derives its name. [16]I pray that out of his glorious riches he may strengthen you with power through his Spirit in your inner being, [17]so that Christ may dwell in your hearts through faith. And I pray that you, being rooted and established in love, [18]may have power, together with all the saints, to grasp how wide and long and high and deep is the love of Christ, [19]and to know this love that surpasses knowledge – that you may be filled to the measure of all the fullness of God. " [20]Now to him who is able to do immeasurably more than all we ask or imagine, according to his power that is at work within us, [21]to him be glory in the church and in Christ Jesus throughout all generations, for ever and ever! Amen.

1 Corinthians 3:9
[9]For we are God's fellow workers. *Other translations say "co-laborers."*

Romans 15:17-19a

[17]Therefore I glory in Christ Jesus in my service to God. [18]I will not venture to speak of anything except what Christ has accomplished through me in leading the Gentiles to obey God by what I have said and done – [19]by the power of signs and wonders, through the power of the Spirit.

XI)There are different levels of healing noted in the New Testament among the members of the church.

A) Role

Matthew 28:20
[20]Teaching them to obey everything I have commanded you . . .
(Healing, deliverance, ministry to the poor, and raising the dead were often the heart of Jesus' commands to the disciples.)

B) Gifting – gifts of healing

1 Corinthians 12:9
[9] . . . to another gifts of healing . . .*(plural 'healings' in the Greek)*

C) Ministry of healing

1 Corinthians 12:30
[30]Do all have gifts of healing?

D) Office of Healer

1 Corinthians 12:28b
[28]. . . also those having gifts of healing . . .

E) Ministry of Working of Miracles

1 Corinthians 12:29
[29]Do all work miracles?

F) Office of worker of miracles

1 Corinthians 12:28
[28]And in the church God has appointed first of all apostles, second prophets, third teachers, **then workers of miracles,** also those having gifts of healing, those able to help others, those with gifts of administration, and those speaking in different kinds of tongues. *(Note that the office of "workers of miracles" is not the same as the office of the apostle (though the apostles did work miracles in this context notice that the office of the Evangelist isn't listed here with the other 4 office gifts. Pastor isn't mentioned either, but many see the pastor/teacher designation as referring to one office with the pastor also being a teacher.)*

XII) Authority and power are connected to the name of Jesus.

(This strengthens the issue of dependence and it not being our resident power that is referred to in these passages, but to an external power that comes as a result of our dependence upon God. The Christian view of God is not compatible with the Hindu or Buddhist understanding of God, or the New Age understanding of God.)

A) Jesus said there would be power in His name

John 14:13-14

¹³And I will do whatever you ***ask in my name***, so that the Son may bring glory to the Father. ¹⁴You may ask me for anything ***in my name***, and I will do it.

John 14:26

²⁶But the Counselor, the Holy Spirit, whom the Father will ***send in my name***, will teach you all things and will remind you of everything I have said to you.

John 15:16b

¹⁶Then the Father will give you whatever you ***ask in my name***.

John 16:23-24

²³In that day you will no longer ask me anything. I tell you the truth, my Father will give you whatever you ***ask in my name***. ²⁴Until now you have not asked for anything ***in my name***. Ask and you will receive, and your joy will be complete.

Mark 16:17-18

¹⁷And these signs will accompany those who believe: ***In my name*** they will drive out demons; they will speak in new tongues; ¹⁸ they will pick up snakes with their hands; and when they drink deadly poison, it will not hurt them at all; they will place their hands on sick people, and they will get well.

B) The record of the New Testament Church reveals there was Power Related to the name of Jesus

Peter says in Acts 3:16

¹⁶By faith in the name of Jesus, this man whom you see and know was made strong. It is Jesus' name and the faith that comes through him that has given this complete healing to him as you can all see.

Acts 4:10

¹⁰Then know this, you and all the people of Israel: It is by the name of Jesus Christ of Nazareth, whom you crucified but whom God raised from the dead, that this man stands before you healed.

Acts 4:30

³⁰Stretch out your hand to heal and perform miraculous signs and wonders through the name of your holy servant Jesus.

Acts 5:40

⁴⁰They called the apostles in and had them flogged. Then they ordered them not to speak in the name of Jesus, and let them go.

Chapter 7: Medical Science Research Pertaining to Healing and Spirituality

Lesson Goals

1) To gain an understanding of the brain effects the physical body (Psychoneuroimmunology defined)
2) To understand the medical implications of belief systems on the brain
3) Understand the historical significance of linking health and religious involvement
4) To review the history of associating healing in the body to beliefs and religious association through recent studies
   - Studies on stress and health
   - Studies on depression and health
   - Studies on religious beliefs and health

Introduction

Throughout the medical community there has been a growing interest in the effects that experience, beliefs, and emotions have on the human body. Emotions, it seems, are the direct result of our belief systems and how they interpret experience. As healing evangelist have come and gone, there has been a nagging question as to whether the healings were a placebo effect, or the result of heightened emotional states. This has caused some to question whether there is an actual lasting change, or whether there is some significance to a supernatural power that is beyond our control, that can bring healing to the physical body. This session is a result of the growing interest in this particular area of study. As Dr. Herbert Benson states in his book *Timeless Healing: The Power and Biology of Belief* (1997:39) "Every specialty and subspecialty of medicine is having to reevaluate and appreciate how intimately our thoughts are related to our bodies".

In this lesson we will not only look at the effect of religious activities and beliefs on the physical body, but also at some of the "unexplainables". By the end this chapter you should have gained a clear understanding of the way emotions and beliefs, when coupled with experience, can promote or hinder a healthy physical body. This will also shed light on the specific effects of religious activity and supernatural healing.

---

1 Corinthians 6:19

Or do you not know that your body is the temple of the Holy Spirit *who is* in you, whom you have from God, and you are not your own? (NKJV)

Preliminary Definitions

In this chapter we will cover some medical terminology that may not be known to everyone reading. In order to better aid this session here are some key terms defined, and general statements explained.

Religious Activity/ Involvement: This primarily speaks to involvement in organized Christianity (Denominational Churches), Judaism, and Islam. It should be assumed that this is the type of activity/involvement meant: regular church attendance, Bible studies, home group meetings, etc., in a traditional religious environment. This is based on Koenig, McCullough and Larson's definition from the *Handbook of Religion and Health,* that religion is more specific and includes "rituals or prescribed behavior" (2001:17)

Studies: Most studies cited in this session will be no more than 15 years old. Some may be older, especially when showing the history of a theory tested. A study is done to show if there is a relationship or correlation between two things. (i.e. smoking and lung cancer).

Placebo Effect: In the simplest terms it the power of suggestion to help the body heal itself. Through mere suggestion the body can exhibit signs of improved health without specific medical intervention. (i.e. "take this pill to help your headache", the pill is really a sugar pill, but the patient no longer has the symptoms of the headache, believing that the pill cured them.)

Key Insights

I)   The chemical and physical effects the brain has on health in the body

A) Psychoneuroimmunology:

Psychoneuroimmunology is "the study of how social and psychological factors affect neuroendocrine and immune functioning" (Koenig and Cohen 2002:11). In a sense it is the overall examination of how such factors as stress, social support, anger, unforgiveness, joy, etc, affect the body's release of certain chemicals that can either help or hinder the health in the body.

B) Stress

Don Colbert, in *Deadly Emotions,* writes about the specific effect that emotions can have to the body that are deadly and need to be treated. He indicates that stress is the number one factor leading to disease in the body (2003:ch 4).

1) Stress Defined:

"Stress is the body and mind's response to any pressure that disrupts their normal balance. It occurs when our perceptions of events don't meet our expectations *and we don't manage our reaction to the disappointment.* Stress – that unmanaged reaction- expresses itself as resistance, tension, strain, or frustration, throwing off our physiological and psychological equilibrium and keeping us out of sync. If our equilibrium is disturbed for long, the stress becomes disabling. We fade from overload, feel emotionally shut down, and eventually become sick." (Colbert 2003:8)

a) Stress causes a constant release of hormones inside of the body. At times this can be used for good, but more often than not this allows for a release of chemicals, or adrenaline

b) The body's cells have a memory that recalls and reacts to the release of adrenaline.

c) *Being in constant states of stress, causes a constant release of adrenaline, only allowing cells to remember/react in one way, leading to constant accommodating by the body.* (Colbert 2001:12-15)

2) Stress Emotions and their Effects (Colbert 2001):

a)	*Anger/Hostility*	High Blood Pressure, Coronary Artery Disease, Major Heart conditions, Back Pain, Ulcers, Headaches
b)	*Depression*	Heart Disease, Osteoporosis, Cancer

c) *Guilt and Shame*	Fibromyalgia, Chronic Fatigue Syndrome
d) *Fear*	Cardiovascular Disease, Hypertension, Digestive-Tract Diseases, Crone's Disease, Ulcers, Headaches, Eczema

II) Timeless Healing: The Power and Biology of Belief

Previously in this session it has been proven that there is a link to emotions/beliefs and the deterioration of health. We will now turn our focus to the ability the body has to heal through positive emotions associated with beliefs, specifically religious involvement. We will look at many of the findings from the book *Timeless Healing: The Power and Biology of Belief*, by Dr. Herbert Benson (1996).

A) Placebo Effect

1) Dr. Henry K. Beecher – 1955 study, with 30% success rate (Benson 1996: Ch. 2)

2) Dr. Alan H. Roberts – 1994 study, 70% success rate (Benson 1996: Ch. 2)

3) Subjective to the change in technology – *The placebo is contingent on the marketing and endorsement of a new drug. Because it relies on the power of suggestion, it is only as powerful as that suggestion.* (Benson 1996: 116)

B) Remembered Wellness

The Three Components of Remembered Wellness

1. Belief and expectancy on the part of the patient
2. Belief and expectancy on the part of the caregiver
3. Belief and expectancies generated by a relationship between the patient and the caregiver
(Benson 1996:32)

C) Relaxation Response

Two Steps of the Relaxation Response

1. Repeat a word, sound, prayer, phrase, or muscular activity

2. Passively disregard everyday thoughts that come to mind, and return to your repetition.
This is suggested to be the most effective when coupled with Remembered Wellness. The originator of these practices, links them together as a way to re-structure, or train the brain to release healing into the body. (Benson 1996:134)

D) Cognitive Restructuring – Thoughts are redirected to interpret life in a more positive way. (Benson 1996:138)

E) Nature versus Nurture - Both are neurosignatures – neither has *dominance* **(Benson 1996:93)**

F) Statistical Findings

1) The Influence of Religious Factors on Health
2) The Influence of Religious Factors on Psychological Measurements

III) Handbook of Religion and Health: Studies Linking the Two

We will now turn our attention to one of the most comprehensive collections of studies linking religious beliefs and health. The following are several categories that showed a significant relationship woven throughout several studies.

A) History of Religion and Health

1) "According to Ferngren (1992, pp. 13-14), caring for the sick was Christianity's truly novel contribution to health care." (Koenig et al. 2001:29)

2) "By the end of the century, more than 60 medical schools (of the 126 schools in the United States) have courses on religion, spirituality, and medicine." (Koenig et al. 2001:49)

B) The Positive Effects of Religion on Health and the Medical Science

1) 1980 – The serious consideration of incorporating religion into psychology (Koenig et al. 2001:57)

2) Lower rates of illness, depression, and unsatisfactory life during the older generations before us – The Buffer of Religion (Jung,1933, p. 229)

C) Coping

1) "Investigators reported that out of 40 possible coping behaviors, pray/trust in God was rated second among hypertensive patients and tenth among other patients" (Jalowiec & Powers 1981). (Koenig et al. 2001:81)

2) African American elderly lean on religion -   One of the two names methods for coping was "Thinking of God or your religious beliefs" (Conway 1985). (Koenig et al. 2001:83)
Religious affiliation was cited as being more important than race and ethnicity amongst these elderly African Americans

D) Mental Illness and Personality

1) Schizophrenia and Psychosis

    a) "…schizophrenia was less common among affiliates of Pentecostal/Holiness groups then among members of other denominations". (Buckalew 1978). (Koenig et al. 2001:157)

    b) Parents of schizophrenics were also less likely to:
-practice family devotions regularly (8% vs. 32%),
-were more likely to teach that God is punitive and harsh (73% vs. 30%),
-and were more likely to teach religion in authoritarian manner (40% vs. 14%). (Koenig et al. 2001:159-160)

2) Personality
General overview of significant correlation found with religious involvement:
    a) Well-being, happiness, and life satisfaction
    b) Hope and optimism
    c) Purpose and meaning in life
    d) Higher self-esteem
    e) Adaptation to bereavement
    f) Greater social support and less loneliness
    g) Lower rates of depression and faster recovery from depression
    h) Lower rates of suicide and fewer positive attitudes toward suicide
    i) Less anxiety
    j) Less psychosis and fewer psychotic tendencies
    k) Lower rates of alcohol and drug use or abuse
    l) Less delinquency and criminal activity
    m) Greater marital stability and satisfaction
    n) "We concluded that, for the vast majority of people, the apparent benefits of devout religious belief and practice probably outweigh the risks." (Koenig et al. 2001:228)

E) Physical Health

Significant links found to religious involvement and

    1)   Hypertension
    2)   Cerebrovascular Disease and the Brain
    3)   Cancer
    4)   Even Mortality
        • "Frequent religious attendance (once or more a week) is associated with a 25-33% reduction in the risk of dying during follow-up periods ranging from five to 28 years. "(Koenig et al. 2001:330)

    5)   Cigarette smoking
        • "If religiousness can help prevent the onset of cigarette smoking during adolescence or young adulthood, people will enjoy the health benefits of avoiding this habit throughout their life-times. Recall that 21% of coronary heart disease deaths, 30% of cancer deaths, and almost all deaths from chronic bronchitis and emphysema could be prevented if Americans never started smoking cigarettes". (Koenig, George, Cohen et al.:1998b). (Koenig et al. 2001:371)

F) Final association of Religion and Health

1) The Great Impact:
   - "In fact, the overall effect of social support on physical health is estimated to equal that of abstention from cigarette smoking"(House, Landis, et al., 1988). (Koenig et al. 2001:392)

2) Live longer – the tie between longer mortality and religious activity.

IV) The Link Between Religion and Health

A) *"How might a health care system, hemorrhaging money yet leaving millions of citizens with inadequate access to care, respond to such an inexpensive therapeutic intervention, whose potential health benefits might be vast and whose costs and side effects are minimal"* (Kaye 1997).

B) The modern health care system as we know could reap the benefits of the proven connection between religion and health. In an instant the argument of universal health care systems, and HMO's could be obsolete, or at least minimized with the recognition and allowance of religion to impact the medical community.

1) Darwinian Viewpoint
2) Psychoneuroimmunology and the unavoidable religious connection

V) Conclusion

A) It is necessary to evaluate the cause of illness to the body outside of infection and virus. In doing this the "cause" allows for the "effect" to be unmasked, and essentially rendered powerless. This occurs when the cause (stress, emotional toxicity, learned response), is tempered and re-taught by repetitious religious behaviors, and social support primarily centered around religious activity.

B) However, there does come a point where it is no longer an act of positive confession, or even the un-explainable effect church attendance has on long life. No matter what a study shows, it is still simply proving that there is a relationship, but it does not get to the heart of that relationship, to the supernatural grace and mercy that is released through that relationship. The studies simply prove what God has been telling us all along: He is sovereign and in him there is life forever more.

Notes

Notes

Chapter 8: New Science and the Implications of Quantum Theory

> **Psalm 24**
>
> 1 The earth is the LORD's, and everything in it,
>
>   the world, and all who live in it;
>
> 2 for he founded it upon the seas
>
>   and established it upon the waters. (NIV)

Lesson Goals

The purpose of this lesson is to review some of the basic principles of physics that have led to our current understanding of the nature of reality, and to provide the tools to discern what is actually "scientific" and what is not.

Introduction

Scientists throughout history have developed an approach to studying problems in an organized fashion. This process is part of what distinguishes credible science from speculation. The Scientific Method is essentially:

Make Observations, Record Data.

Construct an hypothesis to attempt to explain how something works or its nature.

The hypothesis should contain predictions about outcomes consistent with the hypothesis.

Design experiments to test –preferably directly – if the predictions are true.

Evaluate the data.

Confirm the hypothesis, refute the hypothesis, or adjust it to explain the new data.

What Science is not: Opinions, feelings and ideas that cannot be tested either directly or indirectly. However, many of the newer theories in physics are being derived primarily from the implications of mathematical equations. When this happens as the first step in the discovery process, experiments then need to be designed to either prove or disprove the theory.

Our understanding of the physical world is continually growing and changing. Much of what we consider "our world" depends on what we can experience and/or measure. As the ability to detect or measure something (for example energy) improves, our theories will likely change to accommodate the new information.

There are three large categories in the history of science and medicine.

1. The early philosophers like the Greeks, Plato and Aristotle, through medieval times

2. The 17th, 18th and most of the 19th centuries (Age of Reason, Age of Rationalism, and Age of Enlightenment) including Galileo, Sir Isaac Newton, etc.

 3. The emergence of the theories of relativity and quantum physics (late 19th century to the present) including Einstein, Bohr Heisenberg, Oppenheimer, Teller, Feynman, Wheeler, Brian Greene, etc.

This outline will cover the basic world view of the various times and a little of the basic scientific beliefs of those times. Special emphasis will be placed on the basic understandings of matter and energy and on the development of the mathematics that led to the discovery of quantum physics.

Lesson 8 will cover:

A. History of the "Old Science"

    1. Greek philosophers

    2. Classical Mechanics (Newtonian Physics)

B. History of the "New Science" - Relativity and the Quantum

    1. Theories of Relativity

    2. Development of Quantum Mechanics

    3. Applications of relativity and quantum physics

    4. Philosophical implications of relativity and quantum physics

    5. Beyond the new Science - the search for the "theory of everything"

C. Conclusion

Key Insights

Definitions:

Mechanics - the study of motion and the effects of forces on physical objects.

Classical Mechanics - also called Newtonian mechanics – our "cause and effect" world.

Quantum Mechanics - the study of atomic or sub-atomic particles which do not behave like larger particles in our "Newtonian world."

Basic concepts:

Physics and science in general started as philosophy and observation.

Physics has developed into an almost completely mathematical discipline that is best described only in the language of mathematics.

Several physics writers have attempted to explain modern physics in nonmathematical terms to the lay reader.

The conventional world view of a relatively stable "cause and effect" universe has been seriously challenged with the development of the theories of relativity and quantum physics.

"What goes up, must come down" is not necessarily true all of the time.

The special laws of the new physics, however, only apply to very small and very fast particles - objects which are smaller than atoms (smaller than ten billionths of a centimeter) and which move faster than about one tenth the speed of light. (The speed of light is 186,000 miles per second.)

The principles of quantum physics have been demonstrated convincingly, and many new technologies have developed from them.

Just as Newton's laws of motion and gravity are now a special case of quantum mechanics, so the new laws of physics will be a part of some larger theory in the future. We do not yet have the full story.

The potential implications that can be drawn from the actual data have changed people's imaginations and their perceptions of reality and consciousness; however, implications are not facts.

I) History of the "Old Science"

A. The Greek Philosophers

Early Mathematics
Geometry - one of the major contributions of Greek mathematicians

Pythagoras (about 570 B.C.) best known for the theorem about right angled triangles.
Pythagoras founded a religious a cult which believed in a form of reincarnation.
Believed strongly that numbers had a mystical significance.
Believed the universe was somehow constructed from numbers.
Heavenly bodies somehow moved in a perfect harmony, producing music.

Euclid (about 300 BC), compiled a book called <u>Elements</u> which contained all the known geometric theorems at that time. Common geometry is still called Euclidian Geometry.

The concept of atoms:

Democritus (Greek philosopher) - developed the concept that there was a smallest possible piece of basic matter around 460 B.C. He called them atoms.
Aristotle did not agree with the concept so it was lost for centuries.

Aristotle (Greek philosopher 384 - 322 B.C.))
Aristotle developed an organized approach to scientific inquiry. He was considered the greatest thinker of the ancient world. His work informed most of the official scientific beliefs of the Catholic Church for almost 2,000 years. Until the sixteenth and seventeenth centuries most universities were dominated by Aristotelians. For centuries theories and observations that did not conform to Aristotle were denounced as heretical.

Aristotle's father was the family physician of King Philip of Macedonia.

Aristotle established the standard professional approach to scientific research.

His work was based on 1) logical deduction; and 2)empirical observation.

This is in contrast to Plato who believed that mathematical reasoning could arrive at the truth by itself. Plato studied mathematics and metaphysics, while Aristotle also studied the natural world including physics, mechanics and biology.)

Aristotle made detailed observations of about five hundred different animals.

Aristotle's science was based on observation and logic, BUT it was not based on experimental methods.

Aristotle believed that observation of physical phenomena could ultimately lead to the discovery of natural laws governing them. These natural laws were somehow divine in nature.

Basic Concepts:
The universe was divided into two parts -terrestrial (earth) and celestial (heavens).
Celestial was everything beyond the moon including the sun, the stars, and the planets.

Matter was composed of five elements: earth, fire, air, water and quintessence.
The earth was made of earth, fire, air, and water.

The heavens were made of an element called quintessence or aether which was the divine substance of the heavens. It was pure and perfect. (The moon was so near earth that although it was mostly quintessence it also contained some earthly substance as well.)

The natural state of an object was determined by the percentage of elements it contained. Rocks fall to the ground because they are largely earth - smoke rises because it is mostly of air and fire.

Laws governing the motion of objects on earth were different than the laws governing the motion of heavenly bodies.

An object on earth could move as long as there was a force applied to it.

Objects in the heavens were moved because of the action of the Prime Mover (or God or the Unmoved). Since the heavens were made of a perfect substance, stars and planets moved in circular motions because circular motion was more perfect.

Mathematics:
Aristotle formalized the mathematical system of Logic.
He did not attempt to mathematically describe the world because he did not consider mathematics and the world to be significantly related.

Painful transitions
In Aristotle's time the prevailing view was that the earth was the center of the universe. Later these views were challenged by scientists who believed that the earth revolved around the sun. Galileo was tried by the Inquisition for his advancement of the theory of heliocentrism. He was eventually forced to recant his views and remained under house arrest from 1633 until his death in 1642. In 2000, Pope John Paul II issued a formal apology for all the errors of the Church over the last 2000 years including the trial of Galileo.

B. Classical Mechanics (Newtonian Physics)
Mechanics in physics is the study of the motion and the effects of forces on physical objects. Classical mechanics is also called Newtonian mechanics as Newton's Laws of Motion are central to the theory. The study of classical mechanics also includes the work of scientists including Copernicus, Kepler, Galileo and René Descartes.

Basic Concepts:
Space is uniform everywhere from any point of view independent of motion.
Space has 3 dimensions and is continuous - based on the model of Euclid's geometry.
An object's position can be described as a point in space.

Time is uniform. It operates unidirectionally and equivalently everywhere.

If all of the forces acting on an object can be known, then the motion of the object can be calculated.

Motion results from the action of known forces - cause and effect.

If the position and momentum of a particle are known, and if all the forces acting on it are known, then its motion can be known exactly for any time in the future.

Classical mechanics is the "physics" of everyday experience. It can be used to describe all common physical events on earth, the motion of the stars and planets. It is useful for all common applications including space travel.

Classical mechanics describes all objects which are relatively larger than atoms (larger than ten billionths of a centimeter) and which move slower than about one tenth the speed of light. (The speed of light is 186,000 miles per second if measured in a vacuum.)

Classical mechanics breaks down at very small sizes and very fast speeds.

Newton
Sir Isaac Newton (1642-1727) was a British physicist who developed a model of scientific inquiry that is still used today.

Isaac Newton brought together the work of Copernicus, Kepler, Galileo and others to finally overturn Aristotle's description of the universe.

The laws that govern motion in the heavens and motion on earth are the same laws.

Newton developed three general rules about the movement of objects (3 laws of motion).

Newton described universal gravitation.

Newton's mechanics described causal laws of nature. All motion is the result of the action of known forces – Deterministic.

Three Laws of Motion:
Newton's First Law of Motion states that a body in motion remains in motion and a body at rest remains at rest unless an external force is applied to it .

Newton's Second Law of Motion states that there is a relationship between the acceleration, force, and mass of an object.

Newton's Third Law of Motion states that for any action there is an equal and opposite reaction.

Mathematics:

Newton was the co-inventor (with Leibniz) of calculus which he needed to invent in order to solve the problems associated with formulating his laws of motion.

Gravity

Newton developed the law of universal gravitation in 1687.
Each object in the universe attracts every other object in the universe in a manner that can be calculated. He named this attractive force gravity (from the Latin *gravitas* which means "heaviness" or "weightiness.")

Light

Newton demonstrated that white light can be broken into many different colors.

Philosophical Issues the "Clockwork Universe"

Since the motion of objects could now be described so well in terms of cause and effect, some people were led to a more deterministic view of nature. The universe became predictable. God may have been the master builder, but some people concluded that the universe was simply a perfect machine that God decided to set up and just "let it run." (i.e. Deism).

II) History of the "New Science" - Relativity and the Quantum

Some basics concepts to get started:

More Definitions

> **Atoms** - The atom is still the basic building block of molecules as we know them. The atom is composed of a nucleus (positively charged protons plus neutrally charged neutrons) and negatively charged electrons which surround the nucleus at relatively large distances from it. The interaction of electrons is the basis for most chemistry. Electric currents are basically caused by the movement of electrons.

> **Electromagnetism** - involves the relationship between electricity and magnetism. For example an electric current flowing through a wire generates a magnetic field around the wire. The two were considered separate entities until James Clerk Maxwell showed that they were parts of a single phenomena. While studying the nature of light he concluded that light is an electromagnetic wave. He predicted the existence of radio waves.
> In 1873 he published the *Treatise on Electricity and Magnetism*. A changing magnetic field is always related to a changing electric field. Electromagnetic radiation is a spectrum of **waves** from radio waves (the longest) to microwaves, infrared light, visible light, ultraviolet light, X-rays and gamma-rays (the shortest).

> **Forces** - There are four fundamental forces that we know about at this time. They are
> 1) the electromagnetic force, 2) the strong nuclear force which holds quarks together and keeps the nucleus together. (Quarks are even smaller pieces of matter that make up the protons and neutrons in the nucleus of the atom.) 3) the weak nuclear force which is responsible for some forms of radioactive decay, and 4) the gravitational force.

> **Photons** - The photon is the carrier of electromagnetic radiation. It is the mediator for any type of electromagnetic interactions including magnetic fields. The photon travels at the speed of light and has no mass. It does, however, carry energy momentum and has polarization.

History of the atom:

Democritus (460 BC- 370 BC) first postulated the existence of atoms as the smallest piece of a substance. Atoms had : size, shape, and motion.

The first modern notion of the atom came from John Dalton in 1808. His vision of the atom was similar to that of Democritus so he kept the same name. Dalton established that all atoms of a specific element have the same size and weight and that they combine in specific proportions to form other compounds.

Ernest Rutherford was the first to describe the atom as more than a round mass. In 1911 he determined that an atom was composed of a positively charged nucleus surrounded by negatively charged electrons orbiting around it. This was similar to the planets revolving around the sun so his model was called either the nuclear model or the planetary model of the atom.

1905 Albert Einstein published a paper on Brownian motion (the movement of pollen in fluids) which proved of the existence of atoms.

In 1913 Niels Bohr used quantum theory to develop the quantized shell model of the atom. This model could explain how electrons could remain in stable orbits around the nucleus without emitting radiation. This model is still the accepted model for the structure of the atom (more on this below).

The birth of the new science:

Studies on the nature of light, electromagnetic waves and the small particles (atoms and molecules) came together to form what can be considered the "new science" of the 20th century.

Max Plank and the birth of the quantum

By the end of the 19th century, scientists studying electromagnetic radiation, heat, light and atoms were beginning to discover properties that did not behave properly according to the principles of classical mechanics. For example, describing light as a wave could not account for all of the phenomena they were observing. To solve this problem Max Plank proposed in 1900 that the laws of electromagnetism needed to be modified.

According to Plank, electromagnetic wave energy always appeared in packets containing fixed amounts of energy. Energy in each packet is determined by the frequency of the electromagnetic wave and is greater for higher frequencies (i.e. shorter wavelengths). Such a packet of energy is called a "**quantum**" which in Latin means "amount."

A) Theories of Relativity

Einstein and the birth of relativity

Wave-particle duality. In the first of three famous papers published in 1905, Einstein predicted that light can behave like a particle, as well as a wave. Light comes in discrete packages of energy called photons (light particles originally called light quanta). Einstein's theory formed the basis for much of quantum mechanics, and "it is now believed that wave-particle duality is a universal property of all types of particles."* Einstein received the 1921 Nobel Prize in physics for this discovery.

*Alastair I.M. Rae Quantum Physics a Beginner's Guide, Oneworld, Oxford 2005 p36.

Einstein's Special Theory of Relativity - Mass and Energy are related
The second of Einstein's 1905 papers proposed what is today called the Special Theory of Relativity. Mass and energy were equivalent.

$$E=mc^2 \qquad \text{Where m = mass and c = the speed of light.}$$

Einstein developed two theories of relativity – special and general. The special theory is limited to bodies moving in the absence of a gravitational field.

Einstein's Special Theory of Relativity predicted that **time does not flow at a fixed rate**. A moving clock will appear to tick more slowly relative to a stationary clock. This effect is not apparent in everyday life, but it becomes significant at very high speeds near the speed of light. A postulate of Special Relativity is that the speed of light is always the same for all observers, regardless of their motion.

Proof of the existence of atoms
The third of Einstein's 1905 papers provides evidence for the physical existence of atoms through his calculations for Brownian motion (the movement of pollen in fluids).

Einstein's 1905 predictions were verified experimentally in several ways within the first two decades of the 20th century.

General Relativity and the concept of Space-Time
Einstein developed the General Theory of Relativity in 1915. It unifies the theory of Special Relativity and Newton's law of universal gravitation

Gravity is a property of the geometry of space and time.

Gravitational attraction between masses results from the of warping of nearby space and time.

Einstein's theory predicts astrophysical phenomena such as the existence of black holes—regions of space in which space and time are distorted in such a way that nothing, not even light, can escape.

Implications of Einstein's Theories:
Space and time are no longer absolute. The time elapsed between two observers need not be the same. It depends on their relative speeds. So if someone is traveling near the speed of light, time for them will slow down compared to someone on earth. When the traveler returns a person on earth will have aged more than the traveler. This is called time dilation.

Simultaneous events are relative. Events which appear simultaneous to one observer may not appear that way to another observer.

Mass and energy are essentially equivalent.

If matter is converted into energy large amounts of power will be released.

Space and time become unified into space-time.

Gravitational attraction can cause space-time to stretch or shrink.

The Clockwork Universe is not so predictable any more.

B) Development of Quantum Mechanics

Quantum Mechanics or Quantum Theory is the study of atomic or sub-atomic particles which do not behave like larger particles in our "Newtonian world."

The primary language to describe Quantum Mechanics is mathematics.

Key features:
Uncertainty Principle. The Uncertainty Principle was described by Werner Heisenberg in 1927. It states that you can never know both the position and momentum of an object. The act of measuring one variable will change the other. In other words, the act of observing (or measuring) an object affects it's behavior. Position and momentum cannot be measured simultaneously.

Randomness. The behavior of individual particles is random.

Probability. All calculations are predictions of statistical probability and therefore cannot be exact.

Principles of quantum mechanics:
"These three principles – randomness of individual outcomes, alteration of state by measurement, and our ability to calculate probability underpin the conventional interpretation of quantum physics." …

" First, as far as anyone knows, this [movement of individual particles] is a genuinely random process: which path will be followed by any particular particle is completely unpredictable….before quantum physics came along, it was generally believed that strictly causal laws of nature such as Newton's mechanics determined everything, so all motion would be the result of the action of known forces….In the quantum world, however, this no longer holds: randomness and indeterminism are a fundamental property of nature." …

"A second fundamental idea illustrated by particle polarization is that in general a measurement affects and alters the state of the object being measured" …

"A third principle of quantum physics is that, although the individual events occur at random, the probability of their occurrence can be calculated." Alastair I..M. Rae <u>Quantum Physics a Beginner's Guide</u> Oneworld, Oxford 2005 pp. 159-161.

Later developments in Quantum Theory: Entanglement
Entanglement is the concept that once two objects have interacted or come into being together, they somehow become linked or entangled. What affects one of them will simultaneously affect the other even if they are separated by large distances.
Einstein called this "spooky action at a distance."

Spooky or not, the principles of entanglement are being used in actual technology including encryption for secure networks. Entanglement may provide a nearly uncrackable method of communication.

C) Applications of relativity and quantum physics -Quantum theory in practice:
"If successful scientific theories can be thought of as cures for stubborn problems, quantum physics was the wonder drug of the 20th century. It successfully explained phenomena such as radioactivity and antimatter, and no other theory can match its description of how light and particles behave on small scales." Maggie McKee, <u>Instant Expert: Quantum World,</u> 11:18 04 September 2006, NewScientist.com news service.

In spite of the apparent randomness of the world of the very small, quantum mechanics makes extremely accurate predictions and modern technology has been forever changed. Some examples:

Sunglasses: "One property of light is known as 'polarization' An electromagnetic wave is one in which a electric field varies periodically in space and time…..this field points along some direction in space. …A wave in which this direction is horizontal is said to be 'horizontally polarized'…An example of a polarizer is the Polaroid used in the lenses of sunglasses: when randomly polarized light passes through this material, half of it is absorbed while the other half passes through with a definite polarization that is defined by the orientation of the lens.. Thus the intensity of the light is halved, while the colour balance is unchanged because light of all colours is treated the same…" Rae p156-157

Small magnetic fields can be measured
"Superconducting quantum interference device (SQUID) . If a SQUID is placed in a magnetic field, "it can measure the size of the flux … with an error considerably less than one flux quantum ….this accuracy of better that one part in 10,000,000,000 which far exceeds that of any other technique for measuring magnetic field." Rae p134 -136

In 2004 the first transfer of money encrypted by quantum keys was performed.

"Quantum cryptography systems work by checking the polarization of a pair of entangled photons to ensure that a key has not been intercepted. If the polarisations do not match, someone is listening in. This has been made to work over short distances: in 2007, researchers succeeded in sending entangled photons over the 144 kilometres [89 miles] between a telescope in La Palma and another in Tenerife in the Canary Islands…. This week, however, researchers at Toshiba's European laboratory in Cambridge, UK, revealed a device that could extend the technique's range indefinitely." <u>Photon counter lets quantum messages go the distance</u> Paul Marks, *New Scientist,* 18 June 2008.

What quantum mechanics can do – uses in our physical world
-supercomputers
-semiconductors
-computer chips
-nuclear bombs
-quantum tunneling
-quantum transporting

D) Philosophical implications of relativity and quantum physics

Everything is relative.

There is no objective reality.

The presence of an observer changes a system.

As everything is only probable, nothing is certain.

There may be parallel or multiple universes.

All things are interconnected.

The Quantum World "can also be mind-bending. Quantum objects can exist in multiple states and places at the same time, requiring a mastery of statistics to describe them. ... the theory has been criticized for casting doubt on the notion of an objective reality - a concept many physicists, including Albert Einstein, have found hard to swallow....The popular 'many worlds' interpretation suggests quantum objects display several behaviours because they inhabit an infinite number of parallel universes."
Maggie McKee, Instant Expert: Quantum World, 11:18 04 September 2006, NewScientist.com news service.

Gary Zukav In 1979 a very popular book appeared that encouraged the **association of quantum physics with Eastern religions.** *The Dancing Wu Li Masters* advertised itself on the back cover as " 'the Bible' for those who are curious about the mind-expanding discoveries of advanced physics, but who have no scientific background." The title comes from Wu Li - a Chinese word for physics which can be translated as "Patterns of Organic Energy." This book was popular enough to be on the Book of the Month Club and similar lists.
Here is an example of the type of ideas it proposes:

" A new instrument of thought such as is needed to understand ... [physics] ... may not be as much of an obstacle as it first appears. There already exists an instrument of thought based upon an 'unbroken wholeness.' ... These psychologies are what we commonly call 'Eastern religions." p 311-12 Gary Zukav *The Dancing Wu Li Masters: An Overview of the New Physics*, Bantam, New York, 1980

Deepak Chopra is another popular author who expands the notion of physics beyond science to philosophy. He coined the term "**Quantum Healing**" which was the inspiration for therapies such as "Quantum Touch" (see chapter 14).

"Research on spontaneous cures of cancer...has shown that just before the cure appears, almost every patient experiences a dramatic shift in awareness. He knows that he will be healed, and he feels that the force responsible is inside himself but not limited to him – it extends beyond his personal boundaries, throughout all of nature. ... At that moment, such **patients apparently jump to a new level of consciousness that prohibits the existence of cancer....**This leap in consciousness seems to be the key. The word that comes to mind when a scientist thinks of such sudden changes is *quantum*. The word denotes a discrete jump from one level of functioning to a higher level – the quantum leap" ...

Quantum is also a technical term, once know only to physicists...I would like to introduce the term **quantum healing** to describe what happened [to a patient]."

Medicine has not taken the quantum leap, and **the word quantum has no clinical application**... Quantum healing moves away from the external, high technology methods toward the deepest core of the mind-body system. To go there and learn to promote the healing response, you must get past all the grosser levels of the body...and arrive at the... point where consciousness actually starts to have an effect." Deepak Chopra, M.D. *Quantum Healing: Exploring the Frontiers of Mind/Body Medicine*, Bantam Books New York 1989 p17 -20.

E) Beyond the new Science - the search for the "theory of everything"

Physicists are particularly interested in finding a theory that will combine quantum mechanics and gravitational forces.

String theory is the most widely known candidate in the search for a theory of everything.
There are variations called string theory, super string theory and M theory. The basic premise is that everything is composed of vibrating strings or vibrating membranes.

These theories accurately describe the behavior of particles, but so far do not explain the nature of space and time. The theories need to invoke up to 11 or 12 dimensions.

These theories are based exclusively upon mathematics which is not complete. The complex equations only work when they use approximations in their calculations.

Also at this point string theory is so complex that it cannot be tested experimentally.

"Without monumental technological breakthroughs, we will never be able to focus on the time length scales necessary to see a string directly. Physicists can probe down to a billionth of a billionth of a meter with accelerators that are roughly a few miles in size. Probing smaller distances requires higher energies and this means larger machines capable of focusing energy on a single particle…using today's technology we would need an accelerator the size of the *galaxy* to see individual strings."
Brian Greene *The Elegant Universe Superstrings, Hidden Dimensions, and the Quest for the Ultimate Theory* Vintage Books, New York 1999, p215.

III) Conclusion

What exactly IS a "Quantum Leap" (besides being a televisions series)?
Technically the term is inspired by the fact that in the atom an electron moves from one discrete energy level to another. (The change of energy levels is not continuous as would have been anticipated if only classical mechanics had been true.) The change is instantaneous, but it is not necessarily large since a very large change of energy would cause the electron to leave the atom altogether.

This idea has been romanticized to mean a large and abrupt– possibly life changing- change.

At what point does Science become metaphysics?
Concepts can be tantalizing and evocative, but they are based on philosophy and not the science itself.

Because this science is so mathematical, any language used to describe it almost has to move to the philosophical implications.

Open Questions
Was Newton wrong? No. Newtonian mechanics is a subset of quantum mechanics.

Is Quantum Mechanics the whole story? No. Gravity is not explained, so it cannot be the complete and final theory.

Einstein said, "God doesn't play dice."

"Many physicists still regard quantum mechanics as a work in progress. It's not that quantum mechanics makes any wrong predictions, or hasn't been able to cope with particles like quarks, concepts like color, or trillion-volt energies. It's just that the theory seems to lack a rationale. 'How come the quantum?" John Wheeler likes to ask. 'If your head doesn't swim when you think about the quantum,' Niels Bohr reportedly said, 'you haven't understood it.' And Richard Feynman, the brash and brilliant American physicist who understood quantum mechanics as deeply as anyone, wrote: 'My physics students don't understand it either. That is because I don't understand it.' Many physicists believe that some *reason* for quantum mechanics awaits discovery." Kenneth W. Ford, *The Quantum World Quantum Physics for Everyone* Harvard University Press, Cambridge, MA 2004 p98-99.

Ultimately quantum mechanics will be found to be a special portion of some other theory – whether it is some form of string theory or something else. Many physicist believe there must be "hidden variables" which will account for phenomena such as entanglement. Time will tell.

I consider the year 1905 to be a pivotal year in the history of physics, because that was the year that Einstein's theories forever changed our concepts of light and time. I doubt that it is a coincidence that the Welsh Revival was happening at this time followed by the Azusa Street Revival in 1906. The Holy Spirit began manifesting more powerfully and in new ways precisely as physics was opening up to new concepts. Of course that is only my theory….

Notes

Chapter 9: Healing Energy - Whose Energy is it?

Lesson Goals

1. To make clear the different meanings of the term "energy" from a Theistic and a Pantheistic philosophy/theology.
2. To make clear the different schools of thought, religions, and/or groups that have a pantheistic and a theistic understanding of healing.
3. To distinguish between the theistic religions and the uniqueness of the Christian perspective in relationship to Jesus, His work (atonement), His continued work (present intercession), and the energy of the Holy Spirit in Jesus' name for miracles, not just healing. (Judaism and Islam are also theistic religions)
4. To point out the difference in the quantity and quality of the testimonies to healing and miracles in these religions and belief systems.

Introduction

There are many healing practices which use the word "energy" in their vocabulary. Those who come from a Christian healing perspective realize that this energy is coming from sources other than the Holy Spirit. As we delve into this discussion of energy, we will be comparing and contrasting Theistic and Pantheistic philosophies of healing and showing the uniqueness of the Christian perspective. We will come to understand that there are various types of energy both good and bad: natural energy in the creation, normal human energy and energy from angelic and demonic beings. There is nothing which can compare, however, to the power and energy of the Holy Spirit working in and through us.

Key Insights

I) Universal Life Force

A) Universal Soul – Platonism

B) Basic Belief of Pre-Christian era Paganism

C) Basic Understanding of Hinduism

D) Basic Understanding of Buddhism

E) Basic Understanding of Neo-Paganism (New Age)

F) Basic Understanding of Theosophy

G) Basic Understanding of Palmer (founder of Chiropractic in the West – already existed in China and East years before)

H) The Understanding of the human being's soul

I) The Understanding of the human being's energy

J) The Understanding of other spiritual beings

(1) Angels

(2) Demons

(3) Emanations or incarnations from Ultimate Reality

II) Secular – Mechanistic – Atheistic

III) Theistic

A) Muslim

B) Jewish

C) Christian

D) Differences between Theism and Monism or Pantheism

IV) Developing a 21st Century Christian Theology of Healing related to the issue of Energy or power

A) Jesus' Understanding of Healing
(1) How it related Power

(2) How it related to Authority

B) Paul's Understanding of Healing
(1) How it related Power

(2) How it related to Authority

C) The Biblical Understanding of the Human Being
(1) The Human Being's Soul and Spirit – the "image of God"
    a) Eradicated by the Fall (Within Protestantism Emil Brunner)

    b) Marred by the Fall, but not Eradicated or Destroyed
(Traditional view of Protestantism and upheld by Barth, but rejected by Liberalism which saw such potential in humankind.)

(2) The Human Being's energy

    a) Yes, if Marred

    b) Question regarding human capacity to receive energy from outside oneself

c) Question of channeling one's own energy

d) Question of channeling energy from other spiritual realities/beings

e) Question of channeling energy from the Universe

f) Question of carrying or being used by the energy of the Holy Spirit

D) The Biblical Understanding of other Spiritual Beings
1) Angels – didn't fall

2) Demons – fallen angels - traditional - most common view

3) Demons – disembodied spirits of the dead - non-traditional - ministry view

E) Possible Sources of Energy
1) Energy Omnipresent in Creation - Natural

2) Human Energy – Human

3) Spiritual Beings Energy (angels and demons)

4) Holy Spirit's Energy

5) Ability of Humans to work with Spiritual Beings (good and bad)

6) Ability of Humans to work with Energy from Holy Spirit

7) Natural or Normal, psychic or paranormal, spiritual beings, Spirit of God

V) Demonstrations of Energy for Healing and other Miraculous or Super-empirical events

A) **New Age**

B) **Theosophy**

C) **Hindu**

D) **Buddhist**

E) **Islamic**

F) **Jewish**

G) **Christian**

Notes

Chapter 10: My Personal Experience of Healing - Part 1

Lesson Goals

1. To gain a better understanding of the various major streams of healing within Christianity.
2. To challenge the presuppositions of Liberalism, Cessationism, Dispensationalism, and by informing people, schooled in these systems, of the continuation of miraculous power for healing in our day.
3. To encourage faith by "the power of the testimony" for healing.
4. To challenge the technological/tool emphasis for valid testing of the Scientific Method; the limits of science.
5. To emphasize the uniqueness of the human being to experience the spiritual realm, that humans are the best "tool" for perceiving the reality of the spiritual realm.

Introduction

I believe that there are limitations to the scientific method. There are things that are real, are experienced, repeatable (but not consistent), that science hasn't been able to verify primarily because the scientific community has not yet developed the tools to quantify or verify the existence of such realities. For example, there was radiation before there was a Geiger counter to prove it. The law of aerodynamics existed before a plane was built. There were germs before we had a microscope to see them.

I believe the human being has the ability to discern and experience realities that our technological machines have not yet been developed to quantify or verify. But, to deny the human experience of these realities, merely because we don't presently understand the yet to be discovered law that governs them, is intellectual dishonesty. We must not allow the "dogma" of scientism to threaten the discovery of truth in the same way that the "dogma" of religion stood in the way of scientific discovery and truth.

Key Insights

I) Sharing from my experience and interviewing others who received major healings, I have noted three streams of healing and three other types of healing that don't fit neatly within the first three streams running together into the river of divine healing in the Protestant Christian tradition.

A) Gift based – word of knowledge and gifts of healings;

> **1 Corinthians 12:28**
>
> [28] And in the church God has appointed first of all apostles, second prophets, third teachers, then workers of miracles, also those having gifts of healing, those able to help others, those with gifts of administration, and those speaking in different kinds of tongues.

1) Charismatic movement

   a) Odessa, Ukraine woman healed after word of knowledge of a tractor and scythe picture

   b) Sao Paulo – car accident upside down caught by seat belt and problems with back

B) Anointing based – office gift, focused more on the person with strong ministry of healing.

(1) 1906-Classical Pentecostal movement
(2) 1947 Latter Rain movement
(3) 1948 Healing Revival

C) Faith based – here the emphasis is primarily upon the faith of the individual who is sick.

   (1) Faith Cure movement (1872 - 1892)
   (2) Modern day Word of Faith movement.

D) Sovereign healings

   (1) Charlie and the Fireball in worship

   (2) Heidi Baker's healing of drug resistant systemic staph infection
E) Healings due to Angelic interaction/cooperation in the meetings

   (1) Manaus: 8 deaf in one meeting healed & 90% of 10,000 when the angels came in on the left

   (2) Gary Oates on our meeting in Rio de Janeiro, small angel blowing fire into the man's head who had a brain tumor.

F) Healings due to experiencing the "Glory" of God in the meetings.

   (1) Heidi and Rolland's experience with the Glory cloud

   (2) Deaf man in Raleigh, N.C. – Glory cloud

II) Types of Conditions/Illnesses Healed

A) Physical disease – violating the law of God – nutrition, sleep/rest, exercise, posture.

B) Psychosomatic diseases violating the law of God – interpersonal relationships and toxic emotions – bitterness, anger, unforgiveness, fear, envy, jealousy.

C) Disease caused by an afflicting spirit or demonized soul (seat of will and emotions)

D) Accidental Injuries

E) Resurrections (95 in Mozambique alone in about 9 years, most occurred in Islamic Provinces).

III) Case Studies

A) AIDS

(1) Englewood, Florida
(2) Wife and husband in Manaus, Brazil
(3) Woman in Goiania, Brazil

(4) Baby in IRIS orphanage, later adopted

(5) Woman in Maryland, USA Jamie Galloway prayed for healed, called out by Jamie.

B) Blind

(1) Man in Goiania, Brazil – Creative Miracle of corneas and pupils - accident

(2) Blind for 3 years – afflicting spirit (I prayed for her)

(3) Born Blind -

(4) 6 in one meeting in Goiania, Brazil

(5) Woman Blind (Bethlehem, PA 30 years blind) 2007

(6) January 2008 India trip – team of 24 saw 44 blind eyes open in 2 days in poor Hindu villages of India – Timothy Berry, age 22, GSSM student prayed for 3 in a row and Jennifer Brylinski, a 21-year-old student from Messiah College had 14 in one day.

C) Deaf

(1) Born deaf – suburb of Annapolis, Brazil -- girl (I prayed for her)

(2) Born deaf – Volta Redonda – Dennis McCormick prayed for her

(3) 8 deaf in one meeting in Manaus – Angelic help

(4) Boy in Odessa, Ukraine—creative miracle, auditory nerve destroyed

(5) Woman born deaf, healed in Bethlehem, PA 2007

(6) Team of 24 saw 17 deaf healed in 10 days in villages of India and in Hyderabad, February, 2008

D) Cancer

(1) Tony Ellis – Pancreatic Cancer, Louisville, KY 1995

(2) Woman in Manaus, Brazil – grapefruit size tumor fell from her body

(3) Brazilian woman, uncontrollable laughter for about 4-5 hours then vomits up cancerous tumor.

(4) Brain Tumor – Terry Mesplay St. Louis

Notes

Chapter 11 and 12: Understanding World Views of the Different Contemporary Healing Models

Lesson Goals

The purpose of this lesson is to present some of the various healing models currently in use. By understanding some of the fundamental elements of each model and the basic world views underlying them, we will be better equipped to evaluate treatment modalities offered to the present day medical practitioner and the medical consumer.

Introduction

The medical landscape of treatments available to patients today has expanded beyond anything that could have been imagined a few generations ago. As with any expansion of knowledge, we are presented with a double edged sword - there is the possibility of great good and great harm.

The medical model commonly used in the Western world has developed over centuries. The concepts central to experimental testing and clinical trials, while now considered fundamental, are actually fairly recent developments.

There are a few basic reasons why this is true. As with physics, the concepts of medicine grew with the advancement of philosophy and with the development of tools to delve deeper into the nature of the human body and the nature of sickness and disease. The scientific method has enabled the medical and scientific communities to explore biology and chemistry in an organized fashion that has led to incredible scientific discoveries and achievements. It has also led to the compartmentalization of the human body into organs, organ systems, cells and ultimately individual molecules.

The increased ability to go further into the nature of molecular structures has allowed us to design drugs with great specificity. This increases safety in many cases, but it also leads to further compartmentalization. The medical community has such specialized knowledge of particular systems that many of our doctors are now specialists such as cardiologists and neurologists. Because of this we are suffering from a lack of primary physicians.

With the physicians and the medications getting more specialized and the business of medicine getting increasingly commercial, patients are beginning to feel like they are being treated like parts on an assembly line. The whole person is getting left behind in the business of laboratory results, diagnoses and treatment protocols.

The development and public embrace of alternative and complementary medicines has resulted because of several factors. 1) Conventional medical treatment is still not effective for many common diseases. 2) Some people are alienated from the concepts of Western medicine because of their belief that drugs have too many side effects. 3) Some people perceive – often erroneously –that "natural" remedies are safer and they have fewer side effects. 4) As we are learning more about other cultures, people are observing the value of therapeutic modalities from around the world.

The National Institutes of Health (NIH) is a collection of 27 institutes under the US Department of Health and Human Services. This is the nations' medical research agency, and the source of much of the grant money spent on medical research in the United States. The study of alternative and complementary medicines has advanced to the point where one of these institutes is the National Center for Complementary and Alternative Medicine or NCCAM. Some of these methods of treatment are becoming "mainline' and are being offered at many hospitals.

Lessons 12 and 13 will cover

I) Western Conventional Medicine (basically founded in rationalism.)

A) A brief historical overview of some key events that led to modern medical thought including the philosophies underpinning Western allopathic medicine.

B) The rationale behind current drug development.

II) Common complementary and alternative therapies (often based on pantheism or panentheism)

A) What are complementary and alternative therapies?

B) "Energy Medicines" - Reiki, Therapeutic Touch, Healing Touch, Quantum Touch

C) Acupuncture and Chinese Medicine

D) Ayurvedic Medicine

III) A brief look at Christian Science

IV) Final thoughts - What is going on with all of these therapies?

V) Conclusion

Key Insights

Definitions

> **Receptors** – molecules within a cell that bind hormones or other chemical signals (including drugs). The chemical interaction causes physiological changes in the cell.

> **Assay** – an experimental method designed to test for specific responses in a tissue or cell.

> **Pantheism** - the belief that God is everywhere and in everything. Pantheists usually deny the existence of a personal God, but they believe that everything is a unity. Religions which subscribe to a pantheistic belief system include , Hinduism, Buddhism, Monism, Sufism, Theosophy and parts of the New Age Movement.

> **Panentheism** - the belief that God is greater than the universe but is in all things.

> **Qi (chi)**: the Chinese term for the life force, vital energy or biofields of all things – also known ki (Japanese), prana (Indian) or homeopathic resonance. Although believed to be the energy of the universe, the actual existence of qi has not been proved scientifically.

> **Meridian**: a channel or pathway through the body along which qi flows.

I) Western Conventional (Allopathic) Medicine

Basic concepts

There is not a unified world view that informs Western medicine. Ideas have developed from Greek philosophy, humanist philosophy, and rationalistic philosophies as well as Christian philosophies.

Medicine developed from philosophy and observation to an experimental science over 2000+ years.

Medical concepts have grown as technology has provided improved methods of observation and analysis.

Views of the human person range from holistic to mechanistic.

A brief history of medicine can show that the scientific approach we now take for granted is relatively new in human history.

A. History (Some background to demonstrate the development of scientific thought through the ages.)

Note: Much of this information came from Roy Porter's excellent book *The Greatest Benefit to Mankind* W.W. Norton & Company, New York, 1997

(1) The early Greeks
Hippocrates (c. 460 – 377 BC)
The body is viewed as basically healthy until sickness intervenes.
The body is composed of four humors which corresponded to four elements. Yellow bile (Choleric) and Fire, Blood (Sanguine) and Air, Phlegm (Phlegmatic) and Water, and Black Bile (Melancholy) and Earth.
The physician's focus is on clinical observation of the patient.

Hippocratic Oath highlights (Porter p 63)
"I will use my power to help the sick…I will abstain from harming or wrongdoing any man by it."
"I will not give a fatal draught to anyone if I am asked, nor will I suggest such things. Neither will I give a woman means to procure an abortion."
"I will be chaste and religious in my life and in my practice."
"Whenever I go into a house, I will go to help the sick and never with the intention of doing harm…
"Whatever I see or hear, professionally or privately, which ought not to be divulged, I will keep secret…"

Galen (c130 -200 AD)
Galen was the primary medical influence for about 1000 years
Traveled widely and brought back drugs from India and Africa.
Physician to the gladiators and ultimately to the emperors
Believed it was important to gain patient's trust – essential in the healing process
Described psychosomatic conditions

Added anatomy and physiology to Hippocratic medicine
Medical beliefs were based on the dissection of animals
Encouraged blood- letting
Believed blood was formed in the liver
Believed the brain carried *pneuma* (air or vital spirits) through the nerves (which were empty ducts) to the muscles to cause sensation and movement.
Described about 500 drugs - vegetable, animal and mineral

(2) Dark Ages - most scientific knowledge was preserved in the Arabic world

(3) Middle Ages
Medicine was largely based on the ideas of Hippocrates and Galen
Universities were founded in Paris, Bologna, Oxford, and Cambridge.

Archbishop Alphansus, a Benedictine monk, brought lost Greek texts back from Constantinople to Saleno around 1100 AD

Albertus Magnus German Priest around 1200
Taught in Paris (Students included Thomas Aquinas.)
First European since Roman times to use scientific method.
Added concepts such as chemical change which was foreign to the methods of Aristotle.

Roger Bacon (c1214 -1294)
Franciscan monk
Emphasized experimentation as the basis of science.

(4) Renaissance and Reformation
Medical humanists
Translated Greek texts from Arabic and medieval Latin
Hippocrates and Galen "rediscovered" in original translations
Goal was to restore medicine to Greek purity

Paracelsus (Theophrastus Bombastus von Hohenheim b. 1493 -1542)
Encouraged scientific method
World view – Catholic mixed with mystical and esoteric doctrines
Refuted much of Galen
Placed chemistry at center of medicine
Mixed chemical compounds from pure ingredients in standard formulas (a new concept)
Believed that chemical principles explained living processes

Joan Baptista van Helmont (1579 – 1644)
Christian philosophy - "For him chemical analysis was a means of achieving understanding of nature and union with God, the marriage of an enquiring mind with fervent mysticism'" Porter p207
Rejected the Greek concept of "humours"
"Vitalist" – believed all objects were alive
Water was the primary element

William Harvey (1578 -1657)
First to demonstrate circulation of the blood via the heart.
This was a bold change from Galen's belief that blood came from the liver.

Rene Descartes (1596-1650)
Considered the father of modern philosophy
"I think therefore I am."
Believed that medicine is the key to the natural world
Mind – body dualism
"Mind (or soul) was insubstantial and immortal, the source of consciousness" Porter   p217
Matter was tangible and quantifiable
Viewed the body as a machine

Antoni van Leeuwenhoek (1632-1723)
"His pious faith convinced him that the study of nature would demonstrate the existence of an 'All-wise
    Creator' and thus expose atheistic suppositions such as spontaneous generation." Porter p225
Developed the microscope
First person to physically see bacteria

(5) Age of Enlightenment (18th Century)
Reason would create a better future

Albrecht von Haller (1708-1777)
Devout Christian
Father of Experimental physiology
Wrote a systematic physiology textbook
"Man possesses a physical body, analyzable in terms of matter and force, and an immaterial soul" Porter
    p250

Edward Jenner (1749 -1823)
Smallpox vaccine

(6) Advances in the 19th Century
Technology and experimental science expand
Pharmacology established as a discipline
Potential medicines of the times (early 1800s) "morphine, codeine, quinine, cocaine, colchicine, ephed-
    rine, atropine, reserpine and digitoxin" Porter p334
First chair of Pharmacology established in 1847

Justus von Liebig (1803-1873)
Professor of Chemistry
Experimental study of how food was converted into energy
Viewed organism as physio-chemical systems
Systemized laboratory research
"His reductionist agenda of applying physical science to living organisms encouraged promoters of scien-
    tific materialism." Porter 325

Francois Magendie (1783-1855)
Organized experimentation into the action of drugs
Studied nerve physiology
Wrote a formulary for the preparation and use of several alkaloid drugs.

Claude Bernard (1813-1878)
Studied curare a South American poison which killed through muscular paralysis
Concluded that some drugs act at localized sights – not universally throughout the body
This led to the notion of "**receptors**"
Demonstrated that the body can make it's own chemicals

Crawford Williamson Long (1815 –1878)
1842 Performed the first surgical operation with general anesthesia induced by ether.

Louis Pasteur (1822-1896)
Demonstrated that germs can cause infection
Developed immunization therapies -cholera anthrax (for animals)
Developed rabies vaccine for people
"Chance favors the prepared mind"

Robert Koch (1843 -1910)
Koch's Postulates 1882 These are the classic rules to prove an infectious agent causes a particular disease.
"To prove an organism was the cause of any disease it was necessary to demonstrate:
1. That the organism could be discoverable in every instance of the disease;
2. That, extracted from the body, the germ could be produced in a pure culture, maintainable over several microbial generations;
3. That disease could be reproduced in experimental animals through a pure culture removed by numerous generations from the organism initially isolated;
4. That the organism could be retrieved from the inoculated animal and cultured anew" Porter 436

(7) Modern Medicine 20th Century
The last part of the 1900s ushered in the advent of "modern" medicine. We see major developments in the area of medicinal chemistry and the development of pharmaceutical companies. The new physics allowed for the discovery of imaging technologies. Other technological advances allowed for the development of immunization and vaccine technologies. Molecular biology has developed from the discovery of genes to the sequencing of the human genome. The "Scientific Method" is firmly established as the correct approach to experimentation and clinical trials. A few early highlights are listed below.

Wilhelm Conrad Roentgen (1845 –1923)
German physicist
1895 produced and detected x-rays or Roentgen rays.
1901 First Nobel Prize in Physics.
Father of diagnostic radiology.

Paul Ehrlich (1854- 1915)
Hypothesized the "lock and key" model for a toxin to bind to a cell
Developed the chemical affinity theory which is the basis for modern drug discovery
Expanded the idea of "drug receptors"
Synthesized and tested compounds – patented compound 606 (Salvarsan) for syphilis

Gerhard Domagk (1895-1964):
Discovered that Prontosil cured mice injected with a lethal dose of *hemolytic streptococci*
Before this time the treatment for *hemolytic streptococci* had been amputation

First sulfa drug
Nobel Prize in 1939

Alexander Fleming (1881 – 1955)
Identified penicillin in 1928
Birth of modern antibiotics.
Received the Nobel Prize in Medicine in 1945

B) The rationale behind current drug development.

Modern medicine is based primarily on drugs and surgery. Although the first surgical operation using ether as general anesthesia was in 1842, the real development of anesthesia occurred in the 20th century, so surgery has been able to progress rapidly.

The other major development has been the development of pharmaceuticals. The pharmaceutical industry began developing biological assays that would indicate the potential effectiveness of a new drug. This approach was used by Ehrlich (see above) who synthesized and tested over 600 compounds that would bind to and kill bacteria. Finally at compound 606 he found and patented an effective agent which ultimately transformed the treatment for syphilis.

Early assays were targeted towards killing bacteria, but methods have been developed to test for other types of disorders as well. Most pharmacology has been based on finding drugs that will bind to particular cellular receptors and either activate or block them.

What are receptors? The notion of receptors developed throughout the 20th century as the science of pharmacology grew. A receptor is a molecule (usually on the surface of a cell) that interacts specifically with another molecule like a hormone. When the hormone binds to the receptor, a series of cellular events occur that leads to a biological change. For example, there are receptors for insulin and dopamine. Most communication between cells is accomplished through receptors. There is a continual feedback exchange between organs and nerves, etc.

This process works in every cell in the body. Feedback loops for appetite control are another example of receptor-mediated interactions. The theory is that if you block a certain pathway (such as the signals that tell you that you are hungry) the physiological effect will be blocked and you will not want to eat so much. Another common example would be blocking certain dopamine receptors in order to treat schizophrenia.

The advent of molecular biology and the ability to grow individual cells in culture has allowed individual receptors to be expressed in large numbers so a drug assay can screen literally thousands of compounds at a time. When a molecule is found in a chemical library that is a good fit with the receptor, medicinal chemists can then create designer molecules with exquisite specificity for that particular receptor. This is hopefully the basis for drugs with fewer side effects.

A significant problem with this approach to drug design is that interactions in the whole body are not emphasized. Sometimes fixing a "part" is not a complete cure, and the whole person needs to be healed. The effects of a person's belief system do not figure into the equation at all, and yet it is well known that the placebo effect is very real. In many ways the human body is still looked at as a machine, from the Western medical perspective, even though the "quantum revolution" in physics is now over 100 years old.

II) Common complementary and alternative therapies

Basic concepts:

Many complementary therapies are based on pantheism or panentheism.

Intercessory (including Christian Healing) Prayer is also considered a complementary or alternative therapy (an energy medicine) by the NIH.

Alternative therapies are designed to replace conventional therapy.

Complementary therapies are designed to be used in conjunction with conventional therapies.

There are numerous such therapies from vitamins and nutrition to exercise and sun lamps.

The desire for such treatments often stem from the belief that the human person needs to be treated as a complete entity – body, mind and spirit.

A holistic approach to patient care is becoming increasingly popular.

National Center for Complementary and Alternative Medicine or NCCAM is a branch of the NIH specifically designed to test and evaluate many of these therapies.

Treatment modalities from other cultures are being subjected to rigorous testing to evaluate their safety and effectiveness.

Many therapies have been removed from their original cultural contexts and are being tested independent of the philosophical underpinnings of their origins.

In spite of this effort, certain therapies will always be linked to their origins – others will not.

Understanding the philosophical underpinnings of certain therapies will help people choose the ones that are consistent with their theological belief system.

Note: NCCAM has developed several excellent papers which describe the various therapies discussed below. As NCCAM encourages dissemination of this material, several sections below will be taken from their work. The link to each web site is included for each section. Selections from other publications are also included to expand on each particular philosophy/ theology. The general web links to this information are http://nccam.nih. gov/ and http://www.nlm.nih.gov/medlineplus/complementaryandalternativemedicine.html

About the NIH and NCCAM

Complementary and alternative medicine (CAM) therapies originated from a variety of sources and cultures. The government is attempting to rigorously test these treatments in a scientific manner. Their goal is to establish which ones are safe and effective. They do not base decisions as to what is effective from any theological perspective, but they do attempt to describe the world view and historical context for the therapies.

A) What is complementary and alternative medicine (CAM)?

http://nccam.nih.gov/health/whatiscam/

NCCAM defines therapeutic modalities as either:
Complementary – to be used in conjunction with conventional medicine

Alternative – to be used in place of conventional medicine

There is often insufficient scientific evidence to fully understand these therapies. Once a therapy is proven safe and effective, it may move into the category of "conventional" medicine and is used more frequently in hospitals and other clinical settings. The objective of NCCAM is to rigorously test some of these modalities to determine if they are actually scientifically valid.

NCCAM divides CAM practices into five groups:

Whole Medical Systems

Medical approaches that are built upon complete systems of theory and practice. They are from across the world. For example:

Homeopathy (from Europe) - an approach designed to stimulate the body's ability to heal through the use of increasingly dilute substances which in large doses would mimic particular disease states.

Traditional Chinese medicine (TCM - From China) – a system of medicine based on the concept that disease stems from a disruption of the flow of qi (chi) or from an imbalance in the two basic forces of yin and yang . TCM includes the use of herbs and meditation, massage, exercises and acupuncture (more below).

Ayurveda (From India) – tries to integrate body, mind and spirit to prevent diseases by the use of herbs and diet, as well as massage and yoga.

Mind-Body Medicine

These approaches attempt to use the mind to alter bodily systems.

"Mind-body medicine uses a variety of techniques designed to enhance the mind's capacity to affect bodily function and symptoms. Some techniques that were considered CAM in the past have become mainstream (for example, patient support groups and cognitive-behavioral therapy). Other mind-body techniques are still considered CAM, including meditation, prayer, mental healing, and therapies that use creative outlets such as art, music, or dance." http://nccam.nih.gov/health/whatiscam/

Biologically Based Practices

Biologicals including herbs, vitamins, etc.

Manipulative and Body-Based Practices

Chiropractic medicine, massage, etc.

Energy Medicine

Therapies that attempt to manipulate the "energetic fields" which surround the human body. These fields have not been demonstrated scientifically yet, but there is increasing clinical evidence that some of these modalities are effective even though the actual mechanisms are not proven. These will be covered in depth below.

Examples of some of the research from clinical trials funded through NCCAM:

For details see the NCCAM web site - http://nccam.nih.gov/research/results/past/

Drinking Black Tea Shows No Impact on Cardiovascular Risk Factors - February 2008

Chinese Herbal Formula May Be Helpful for Peanut Allergies - June 2007

Acupuncture May Help Symptoms of PTSD - June 2007

Meditation May Make Information Processing In the Brain More Efficient - June 2007

Study Compares Year-Long Effectiveness of Four Weight-Loss Plans - March 2007

Garlic Does Not Appear to Lower "Bad" Cholesterol - February 2007

Omega-3 fatty acids may be helpful in psychiatric care - December 2006

Turmeric and Rheumatoid Arthritis Symptoms - March 2006

B) "Energy Medicines" - Touch Therapies
Therapeutic touch, Healing Touch, Quantum Touch, Reiki

World Views

The world view of these energy medicines is largely based on pantheism or panentheism of one form or another. Intercessory prayer, of course, is based on the theology of the person praying.

The basis for most energy approaches is ultimately the belief in some sort of vital force which we currently cannot measure. It is the common outlook that this energy or vital force permeates the universe and is available to be tapped or channeled to help people heal. Since many of these approaches appear to be effective at some level people have attempted to take the concepts and remove them from their original religious contexts and "Westernize" them or make them purely rationalistic and scientific.

The basic theory of vital energy, life force or biofields is ultimately grounded in the Chinese/ Japanese concept of qi (chi) or ki and the similar Ayurvedic (Indian) concept of prana. It is also know as homeopathic resonance. The belief is that all life and the universe is infused with this energy and when it's flow is disrupted in people the result is disease. The therapies are designed to restore normal flow and to maintain balance and harmony.

These therapies have gained considerable credence in the popular mind due to the advent of quantum physics (see the discussion of "Quantum Healing in Chapter 13). Although the science of quantum physics does not prove energy medicine at this time, it is providing instruments such as the SQUID (superconducting quantum interference device) which may at least help resolve some of the questions by allowing us to definitively measure such energies if they exist.

More importantly, however, the concepts of physics and their potential (though unproven) implications have aroused such imagination that types of "Quantum Healing" are believed to be scientific fact. It is evocative, but not accurate science at this time. In this type of literature the concept of "consciousness" is assumed to apply at the most basic levels so that individual cells can "choose" certain responses.

The use of clinical trials will determine if the energy therapies work, but even demonstrated efficacy will not prove that the background theory is correct. In science it is much easier to demonstrate that a phenomena exists than to explain its mechanism of action. (See the discussion of placebo below.)

About "Energy" - NCCAM divides energy medicines into two types

Veritable – energies that can be measured such as sound, electromagnetic or light. These forces are understood by modern physics.

Putative – energies which may exist but cannot be measured reproducibly with current technologies.

This excerpt is from the NCCAM Backgrounder Energy Medicine: An Overview
http://nccam.nih.gov/health/backgrounds/energymed.htm

"Examples of practices involving putative energy fields include:

• Reiki and Johrei, both of Japanese origin

• Qi gong, a Chinese practice

• Healing touch, in which the therapist is purported to identify imbalances and correct a

client's energy by passing his or her hands over the patient

• Intercessory prayer, in which a person intercedes through prayer on behalf of another"

"In the aggregate, these approaches are among the most controversial of CAM practices because neither the external energy fields nor their therapeutic effects have been demonstrated convincingly by any biophysical means. Yet, energy medicine is gaining popularity in the American marketplace and has become a subject of investigations at some academic medical centers. A recent National Center for Health Statistics survey indicated that approximately 1 percent of the participants had used Reiki, 0.5 percent had used qi gong, and 4.6 percent had used some kind of healing ritual."

"Many small studies of Therapeutic Touch have suggested its effectiveness in a wide variety of conditions, including wound healing, osteoarthritis, migraine headaches, and anxiety in burn patients. In a recent meta-analysis of 11 controlled Therapeutic Touch studies, 7 controlled studies had positive outcomes, and 3 showed no effect; in one study, the control group healed faster than the Therapeutic Touch group. Similarly, Reiki and Johrei practitioners claim that the therapies boost the body's immune system, enhance the body's ability to heal itself, and are beneficial for a wide range of problems, such as stress-related conditions, allergies, heart conditions, high blood pressure, and chronic pain. However, there has been little rigorous scientific research. Overall, these therapies have impressive anecdotal evidence, but none has been proven scientifically to be effective."

Individual Touch Therapies 1.- Therapeutic Touch

from http://www.therapeutictouch.org/

Developed by Dora Kunz and her student Dolores Krieger PhD, RN in 1972.

"The practice is based on the assumptions that human beings are complex fields of energy, and that the ability to enhance healing in another is a natural potential."

"Therapeutic Touch (TT) is used to balance and promote the flow of human energy. It is taught in colleges around the world and has a substantial base of formal and clinical research."

"Therapeutic Touch started at Pumpkin Hollow Farm, a family camp and spiritual retreat center of the Theosophical Society....Dora's abilities extended beyond the usual sense perception. For example, she was particularly known for her work with the unseen human field energies in an individual."

From: *The Spiritual Dimension of Therapeutic Touch* Dora Kunz with Dolores Krieger, PhD, R.N. , Bear & CO. Rochester, VT 2004

Dora Kunz was the former president of the Theosophical Society of America a "world-class clairvoyant." p1

First of this type of healing modality taught as an "intrinsic part of a fully accredited graduate curriculum of a college or university. (New York University in 1975 in a masters-level course called 'Frontiers in Nursing") p2

"We put before the students of TT the idea that we all belong to a greater universe than is apparent, of which peace and order are characteristic. We felt that there is a universal healing field that touches all people, and that having a specific religious belief was important only to the individual healer. Therapeutic Touch, therefore, is not based on a religion; it has no religious background. Until this day, neither Dolores nor I feel that the ability to heal is confined to one religious belief system." p8.

"Therapeutic Touch...has never achieved instantaneous healing, and that was never our purpose....While absolute cure is rare, the conditions of most people have improved and after a while they have regained their health as their own powers of regeneration have strengthened and their immune systems has become more efficient.... Before TT was started, no public hospital would ever allow healing." p8-9

"We believe that there is a healing power with a consciousness that helps you as you pick up the symptoms in the Therapeutic Touch assessment. The idea of a consciousness that understands the circumstances of an individual's illness is foreign to Western Culture..." p97

"Relationships between angels and human beings occur most naturally at that profound level of consciousness that is in touch with the inner self. ...During TT sessions these intelligences can come to a therapist's aid if several conditions are met: the communication itself must be clear, compassionate concern for the healee's well-being must be strong, the intentionality of the healing act needs to be explicit, the healee's karma must allow it, and the need must be urgent for nonordinary intervention. ... the TT therapist should first try her utmost to help or to heal the ailing person, and to think of the angels as supportive background for what she, herself, can do....While not part of the teachings of Therapeutic Touch, Dora's insights regarding angels and humanity clarify much of the healing experience for the TT therapist of compassionate intent." p218-221

Individual Touch Therapies 2. - Healing Touch

From: http://www.healingtouchinternational.org/index.php

"Healing Touch is an "energy therapy," one of many techniques and practices - including acupuncture and yoga - that subscribe to the ancient Eastern concept of energy flow along pathways in and around the body. In this tradition, a flow of energy through the body that's chaotic, blocked, or out of balance is associated with pain, disease, and emotional distress."

Founded by Janet Mentgen, RN in 1989 as a continuing education program for nurses, other health care professionals, and lay persons.

Currently being taught in universities, medical and nursing schools, and other settings internationally.

From Healing Touch Notebook Level 1 Official Notebook for the Healing Touch Certification Program

2007:

"Disclaimer "The Healing Touch Program curriculum and techniques are based upon healing arts concepts and holistic principles including acknowledgment of the spiritual dimension of human life. Practitioners and instructors of Healing Touch engage in a myriad of spiritual practices and come from backgrounds of all the major world religious streams…spiritual principles are addressed in a generic way in order to hold universal appeal. No specific religious or spiritual belief is taught or promoted in the Healing Touch Program".

"Definition of Healing Touch

Healing Touch is a biofield therapy that is an energy-based approach to health and healing. It uses touch to influence the human energy system, specifically the energy field that surrounds the body and the energy centers that control the energy flow from the energy field to the physical body. These non-invasive techniques utilize the hands to clear, energize, and balance the human and environmental energy fields thus affecting physical, mental, emotional, and spiritual health and healing. It is based on a heart-centered caring relationship in which the practitioner and client come together energetically to facilitate the client's health and healing." p12

"Theoretical Basis for Healing Touch

Healing Touch is a philosophy, a way of caring, and a sacred art….This healing is done through the centered heart, thus a spiritual process is established….The practitioner's self-growth is important in the evolution of her or his ability to enable healing." p18- 19

Recommended Book List for Quantum Physics Includes:

Dancing WuLi Masters Gary Zhkav   *Quantum Healing* Deepak Chopra

Individual Touch Therapies 3. – Quantum Touch

From: http://www.quantumtouch.com/index.php?option=com_content&view=article&id=3

Founded by Richard Gordon

How Does Quantum-Touch Energy Healing Work?

"In principal the Quantum-Touch practitioner learns to focus and amplify life-force energy ("Chi" or "Prana") by combining various breathing and body awareness exercises."

"Quantum-Touch uses resonance and entrainment to facilitate healing. The practitioner learns to raise his or her vibration and create a high level of energy. If that energy field is placed around an area of pain, stress, inflammation, or disease, that part of the body will entrain to the higher frequency and allow one's own biological intelligence to do whatever healing it deems necessary."

Why the name "Quantum-Touch?"

"I call the work Quantum-Touch because of the awareness that we're actually dealing with the quantum, subatomic level of life. When Deepak Chopra wrote, " In order for consciousness to affect matter, it must affect it at a quantum or subatomic level."

"We believe that what we're doing is affecting matter on that quantum, subatomic level and it works its way up through the atoms, the molecules, the cells, the tissue"

Individual Touch Therapies 4. - Reiki

1. Reiki Excerpts From NCCAM: http://nccam.nih.gov/health/reiki/

Backgrounder NCCAM: An Introduction to Reiki

Reiki (pronounced "ray-kee") is an energy medicine practice that originated in Japan. In Reiki, the practitioner places his hands on or near the person receiving treatment, with the intent to transmit ki, believed to be a life-force energy.

Key Points

• People give and receive Reiki for various health purposes.

• It is not fully known whether Reiki influences health and how it might do so. The existence of ki has not been proven scientifically.

• The National Center for Complementary and Alternative Medicine (NCCAM) is sponsoring studies to find out more about Reiki's effects, how it works, and diseases and conditions for which it may be most helpful.

Reiki as an Energy Medicine Therapy

The word Reiki is made up of two Japanese words: Rei, or universal spirit (sometimes thought of as a supreme being), and ki.

Thus, the word Reiki means "universal life energy."

A Description of Reiki

Reiki is a therapy that the practitioner delivers through the hands, with intent to raise the amount of ki in and around the client, heal pathways for ki, and reduce negative energies.

When a practitioner performs Reiki, usually the client sits or lies comfortably, fully clothed. The practitioner places her hands on or slightly above the client's body, using 12 to 15 different hand positions, with the intent to transmit ki. … Each hand position is held until the practitioner feels that the flow of energy has slowed or stopped, typically about 2 to 5 minutes. <u>Some Reiki practitioners believe they are helped by "spirit guides" for proper flow of the energy.</u>

More About Ki

People who believe in the existence of ki hold that ki:

• Is spiritual in origin

• Makes up and moves through all living things

• Is available in infinite quantities, positive in nature, and important to all aspects of health

• Is present both inside the body and on its surface

• Flows throughout the body in specific channels

• Has its flow disturbed by negative thoughts or feelings

They also believe that if ki's flow is disrupted, the body's functioning becomes disrupted, and health problems can occur.

Use for Health Purposes

People have sought Reiki treatment for a wide variety of health-related purposes. Some examples include:

• Effects of stress

• Chronic pain

• Recovery from surgery and anesthesia

• Side effects of chemotherapy and radiation therapy for cancer

• Lowering heart rate

• Improving immunity

• Mental clarity

• Sense of well-being and/or spirituality

• Enhancing the sense of peace in people who are dying

A recent national survey on Americans' use of CAM found that 1.1 percent of the 31,000 participants had used Reiki in the year before the survey.

Effects of Reiki

Clients may report a deep feeling of relaxation after a Reiki session. Relaxation in and of itself may have beneficial health-related effects, such as reducing pain, nausea, and fatigue. A client might also experience warmth, tingling, sleepiness, refreshment, and/or the easing of one or more other symptoms after treatment.

Reiki appears to be generally safe, and serious side effects have not been reported. Some practitioners advise caution about using Reiki in people with psychiatric problems.

Sometimes a Reiki client experiences what practitioners call a "cleansing crisis." The person may have symptoms such as a feeling of weakness or tiredness, a headache, or a stomachache. Reiki practitioners believe that these are effects of the body releasing toxins. They advise the client on how to deal with such symptoms if they occur, such as by getting more rest, drinking plenty of water, or eating a lighter diet.

History of Reiki

There are different beliefs about the origin of Reiki—one is that it is based on Tibetan sutras (texts of Buddhism) written by monks. Sources agree that … Dr. Mikao Usui, a Japanese physician and monk, developed this healing approach and spiritual path, named it Reiki, trained others in it, and developed an organization.

Training, Licensing, and Certification

A person does not need a special background or credentials to receive Reiki training.

There are a number of different schools of Reiki. Usually there are three or four levels (or degrees) of expertise, depending upon the school or type. Each level begins with an attunement, or initiation into that level. Receiving an attunement is believed to bring the ability to access Reiki energy and to open what is conceived as a central core of energy in the body.

Training for each level typically takes 1 or 2 days.

Some Points of Controversy

As in other CAM therapies, there are areas of controversy in Reiki. For example:
• Since little is known scientifically about Reiki, accepting its teachings about its healing properties and about ki is a matter of faith.

• Some people believe that effects attributed to Reiki occur for psychological reasons (such as the placebo effect or suggestibility), or that there are no true effects.

• Some people feel Reiki is incompatible with their religious or spiritual beliefs.

• Government licensing and regulation of Reiki practice is a controversial area.

2. From: *Reiki Energy Medicine* Libby Barnett and Maggie Chambers Healing Arts Press Rochester, VT 1996

"With Reiki there is no body manipulation, only physical touch inspirited by universal life energy…..Reiki combines the healing power of touch with life-force energy, made available to the student through a series of initiations that serve to balance and fine-tune the student's personal energy fields….The four initiations are given by a Reiki master, connecting those who receive them to the lineage of Dr. Usui. Once you have been initiated, universal life energy is consistently available to you, because the initiation raises the frequency of the vibratory rate of your personal energy field to a higher level: a level where healing can occur at every moment." p6

The Reiki practitioner conducts vital energy from the universal energy field into the human energy field, where the energy is transmuted into a form that is usable; at the cellular level…Unlike other forms of energy medicine, Reiki does not involve diagnosing imbalance in the recipient's energy field or intentionally repatterning the system There is no possibility of misdiagnosis or energy overload with Reiki… It happens independently of belief system, emotional state, or religious preference. The body's inner intelligence orchestrates the entire session in accordance with the creative intelligence of the universe." p22

"Because your cells contain universal life force, they remember the truth of who they are as they pull in the healing energy. Thus your entire being begins to vibrate with this creative power instead of resonating with the self-limiting pattern. … most of us were not raised with the awareness that we *are* universal life force and that *everything* is energy." p48

3. From: *Reiki for Dummies,* Nina L. Paul, PhD, Wiley Publishing, Inc. Hoboken, NJ 2006

"Reiki comes from a higher source –call it God, higher power, creator, or spirit. A series of simple initiations turns on your Reiki 'light switch,' which gives you the lifelong ability to channel Reiki energy." p1

"What is unique about Reiki is that it opens your energy channels to receive this high-level energy quickly and with no effort on your part." p108

Reiki uses symbols as well as touch. The second symbol "originated from a 'seed syllable' or meditative form … The symbol calls upon the Buddhist deity …who is the Buddha of Infinite Light and Life." p117

"Some Western Reiki teachers take you on a meditation to meet your Reiki guides. It's believed that everyone has spirit guides watching over and helping out. You might envision these figures as saints, gods, angels or masters from your own religion. After you become attuned to the Reiki energy, you might sense or request the help of other guides such as Mikao Usui…certain guides come to you specifically to aid you in Reiki. The purpose of a meditation to meet your Reiki guides is to introduce yourself to these beings." p130

"You are being guided during a Reiki session, and you receive that guidance through your intuition." p137

4. From: *Beginner's Guide to Reiki,* David F. Vennells, Barnes & Nobel New York 1999"

" Many Reiki practitioners from both religious and nonreligious backgrounds have noticed their spiritual lives renewed or reborn as a result of Reiki, almost as if Reiki has the ability to lead people, if they wish, to a deeper awareness of their own spirituality…there are many facets to Reiki, it is not just an Energy. In fact, this suggests that Reiki possesses wisdom and compassion or that Reiki is an expression of a level of consciousness whose essence is complete wisdom and compassion." p4-5

"Reiki can never be used for a negative purpose because it only works for the greatest good. Positive energy can only be used for a positive purpose. If our Reiki intentions are motivated by negative selfishness, they will simply not be fulfilled." p64

[This is a description of one person receiving a third degree attunement] " I was aware that she was beginning to attune me…I was aware of what felt like a funnel to my right and through this opening groups of symbols were arising and surrounding me. I felt so deeply blessed…my Master…said that shortly before the attunement she had been told by one of her spiritual guides that it was the right time to do the attunement….I am eternally grateful to the divine Reiki Masters for using me as a channel for Reiki". p192

Author's note: The subject of the touch therapies is quite controversial both within the medical community and within the Christian community. There are certain people who would consider themselves dedicated Christians who try to help suffering people through Reiki and the touch therapies.

Several Christian Reiki practitioners have told me that they believe the Holy Spirit is the source of their healing abilities. They believe that they are "channeling" the Holy Spirit. I asked another Reiki practitioner if she believed that Christians were channeling something different than a non-Christian practitioner, and I was told that it is all the same energy.

These therapies- especially Reiki - are being advertised by hospitals in New England as serious treatment options. The hospitals do not consider these therapies in any way religious. Some Christians would like to see Christian Healing Prayer given the same respect by these hospitals and hope that the medical community will become more familiar with the importance of this work.

C) Acupuncture and Chinese medicine

(1) Acupuncture Excerpts From http://nccam.nih.gov/health/acupuncture/

Backgrounder: An Introduction to Acupuncture
This publication is not copyrighted and is in the public domain.
Duplication is encouraged.
National Institutes of Health   U.S. Department of Health and Human Services

Acupuncture is among the oldest healing practices in the world. As part of traditional Chinese medicine (TCM), acupuncture aims to restore and maintain health through the stimulation of specific points on the body.

Key Points

• Acupuncture has been practiced in China and other Asian countries for thousands of years.

• Scientists are studying the efficacy of acupuncture for a wide range of conditions.

• Relatively few complications have been reported from the use of acupuncture. However, acupuncture can cause potentially serious side effects if not delivered properly by a qualified practitioner.

About Acupuncture

The term "acupuncture" describes a family of procedures involving the stimulation of anatomical points on the body using a variety of techniques. The acupuncture technique that has been most often studied scientifically involves penetrating the skin with thin, solid, metallic needles that are manipulated by the hands or by electrical stimulation.

Practiced in China and other Asian countries for thousands of years, acupuncture is one of the key components of traditional Chinese medicine. In TCM, the body is seen as a delicate balance of two opposing and inseparable forces: yin and yang. Yin represents the cold, slow, or passive principle, while yang represents the hot, excited, or active principle. According to TCM, health is achieved by maintaining the body in a "balanced state"; disease is due to an internal imbalance of yin and yang. This imbalance leads to blockage in the flow of qi (vital energy) along pathways known as meridians. Qi can be unblocked, according to TCM, by using acupuncture at certain points on the body that connect with these meridians. Sources vary on the number of meridians, with numbers ranging from 14 to 20.

One commonly cited source describes meridians as 14 main channels "connecting the body in a weblike inter-connecting matrix" of at least 2,000 acupuncture points.

Acupuncture became better known in the United States in 1971, when New York Times reporter James Reston wrote about how doctors in China used needles to ease his pain after surgery. American practices of acupuncture incorporate medical traditions from China, Japan, Korea, and other countries.

Acupuncture Use in the United States

The report from a Consensus Development Conference on Acupuncture held at the National Institutes of Health (NIH) in 1997 stated that acupuncture is being "widely" practiced—by thousands of physicians, dentists, acupuncturists, and other practitioners—for relief or prevention of pain and for various other health conditions. According to the 2002 National Health Interview Survey—the largest and most comprehensive survey of CAM use by American adults to date—an estimated 8.2 million U.S. adults had ever used acupuncture, and an estimated 2.1 million U.S. adults had used acupuncture in the previous year.

Status of Acupuncture Research

There have been many studies on acupuncture's potential health benefits for a wide range of conditions. Summarizing earlier research, the 1997 NIH Consensus Statement on Acupuncture found that, overall, results were hard to interpret because of problems with the size and design of the studies.

In the years since the Consensus Statement was issued, the National Center for Complementary and Alternative Medicine (NCCAM) has funded extensive research to advance scientific understanding of acupuncture. Some recent NCCAM-supported studies have looked at:

•Whether acupuncture works for specific health conditions such as chronic low-back pain, headache, and osteoarthritis of the knee

• How acupuncture might work, such as what happens in the brain during acupuncture treatment

• Ways to better identify and understand the potential neurological properties of meridians and acupuncture points

• Methods and instruments for improving the quality of acupuncture research.

2. From: Acupuncture Analgesia: I. The Scientific Basis, Wang, et al, Pain Medicine, 2008.

"Based upon the results of well- designed and appropriately controlled clinical trials, the National Institutes of Health (NIH) in November 1997, issued a statement that supported the efficacy of acupuncture for specific conditions, such as pain, nausea, and vomiting. In 1998, acupuncture became the most popular complementary and alternative medicine modality prescribed by Western physicians."

"Western theories are primarily based on the presumption that acupuncture induces signals in afferent nerves that modulate spinal signal transmission and pain perception in the brain." [In other words acupuncture somehow stimulates changes in the pain perceiving nerves in the body.]

Brain signals for pain are blocked and molecules like endorphins [the neurotransmitters that generate euphoric feelings like "runners high"] are released in the process. Acupuncture "induces analgesic effect via modulation of both the sensory and emotional aspects of pain processing." This review shows brain scanning images which detail which areas of the brain are affected with particular treatments.

D) Ayurvedic Medicine

Excerpts From: http://nccam.nih.gov/health/ayurveda/

This publication is not copyrighted and is in the public domain.

Duplication is encouraged.

National Institutes of Health   U.S. Department of Health and Human Services

Backgrounder: What is Ayurvedic Medicine?

Key Points

• The aim of Ayurveda is to integrate and balance the body, mind, and spirit. This is believed to help prevent illness and promote wellness.

•In Ayurvedic philosophy, people, their health, and the universe are all thought to be related. It is believed that health problems can result when these relationships are out of balance.

•In Ayurveda, herbs, metals, massage, and other products and techniques are used with the intent of cleansing the body and restoring balance. Some of these products may be harmful when used on their own or when used with conventional medicines.

What is Ayurvedic medicine?

Ayurvedic medicine is also called Ayurveda. It is a system of medicine that originated in India several thousand years ago. The term Ayurveda combines two Sanskrit words—*ayur*, which means life, and *veda*, which means science or knowledge. Ayurveda means "the science of life."

Ayurveda aims to integrate and balance the body, mind, and spirit (thus, some view it as "holistic"). This balance is believed to lead to contentment and health, and to help prevent illness. However, Ayurveda also proposes treatments for specific health problems, whether they are physical or mental. A chief aim of Ayurvedic practices is to cleanse the body of substances that can cause disease, and this is believed to help reestablish harmony and balance.

What is the history of Ayurvedic medicine?

Ayurveda is based on ideas from Hinduism, one of the world's oldest and largest religions. Some Ayurvedic ideas also evolved from ancient Persian thoughts about health and healing.

Ayurveda has long been the main system of health care in India, although conventional (Western) medicine is becoming more widespread there, especially in urban areas. About 70 percent of India's population lives in rural areas; about two-thirds of rural people still use Ayurveda and medicinal plants to meet their primary health care needs.

What major beliefs underlie Ayurveda?

Interconnectedness

Ideas about the relationships among people, their health, and the universe form the basis for how Ayurvedic practitioners think about problems that affect health. Ayurveda holds that:

• All things in the universe (both living and nonliving) are joined together.

• Every human being contains elements that can be found in the universe.

• All people are born in a state of balance within themselves and in relation to the universe.

• This state of balance is disrupted by the processes of life. Disruptions can be physical,

emotional, spiritual, or a combination. Imbalances weaken the body and make the person

susceptible to disease.

• Health will be good if one's interaction with the immediate environment is effective

and wholesome.

• Disease arises when a person is out of harmony with the universe.

Constitution and Health

Ayurveda also has some basic beliefs about the body's constitution. "Constitution" refers to a person's general health, how likely he is to become out of balance, and his ability to resist and recover from disease or other health problems. An overview of these beliefs follows.

• The constitution is called the prakriti. The prakriti is thought to be a unique combination of physical and psychological characteristics and the way the body functions. It is influenced by such factors as digestion and how the body deals with waste products. The prakriti is believed to be unchanged over a person's lifetime.

• Three qualities called doshas form important characteristics of the constitution and control the activities of the body. Practitioners of Ayurveda call the doshas by their original Sanskrit names: vata, pitta, and kapha. It is also believed that:

• Each dosha is made up of one or two of the five basic elements: space, air, fire, water,

and earth.

• Each dosha has a particular relationship to body functions and can be upset for

different reasons.

• A person has her own balance of the three doshas, although one dosha usually is prominent. Doshas are constantly being formed and reformed by food, activity, and bodily processes.

In summary, it is believed that a person's chances of developing certain types of diseases are related to the way doshas are balanced, the state of the physical body, and mental or lifestyle factors.

How does an Ayurvedic practitioner treat health problems?

The practitioner will develop a treatment plan and may work with people who know the

patient well and can help. This helps the patient feel emotionally supported and comforted, which is considered important.

Practitioners expect patients to be active participants in their treatment, because many

Ayurvedic treatments require changes in diet, lifestyle, and habits. In general, treatments use several approaches, often more than one at a time. The goals of treatment are to:

• Eliminate impurities. A process called panchakarma is intended to be cleansing; it focuses on the digestive tract and the respiratory system.

• Reduce symptoms. The practitioner may suggest various options, including yoga exercises, stretching, breathing exercises, meditation, and lying in the sun. The patient may take herbs (usually several), often with honey, with the intent to improve digestion, reduce fever, and treat diarrhea. Sometimes foods such as lentil beans or special diets are also prescribed. Very small amounts of metal and mineral preparations also may be given, such as gold or iron. Careful control of these materials is intended to protect the patient from harm.

• Reduce worry and increase harmony in the patient's life. The patient may be advised to seek nurturing and peacefulness through yoga, meditation, exercise, or other techniques.

•Help eliminate both physical and psychological problems. Vital points therapy and/or massage may be used to reduce pain, lessen fatigue, or improve circulation. Ayurveda proposes that there are 107 "vital points" in the body where life energy is stored, and that these points may be massaged to improve health.

III) Christian Science

Mary Baker Eddy (1821-1910) Discoverer of Christian Science

1875 - *Science and Health with Key to the Scriptures*

1879 - Founded the Church of Christ, Scientist, in Boston, Massachusetts,

1908 - Started The Christian Science Monitor

About Mary Baker Eddy:

From http://www.marybakereddylibrary.org/marybakereddy/life.html

"A turning point occurred in 1866 when a severe fall on an icy sidewalk left her in bed in critical condition. … She asked for her Bible and, while reading an account of Jesus' healing, found herself suddenly well. Eventually, she referred to this as the moment she discovered Christian Science. This led to nine years of intensive scriptural study, healing activity, and teaching, culminating in the publication of *Science and Health* in 1875. In this book she marked out what she understood to be the "science" behind Jesus' healing method. As she saw it, his works were divinely natural, and repeatable. Disappointed that existing Christian churches would not embrace her discovery, Mrs. Eddy started her own. In 1879 she secured a charter for the Church of Christ, Scientist, established "to commemorate the word and works of our Master, which should reinstate primitive Christianity and its lost element of healing.""

Key Points

Jesus is not God.

Jesus revealed the Kingdom of God.

God can be understood as light, truth and love.

Reality is centered in spirit.

Material existence is not real.

Evil, disease, sin and death are not real.

Sin is not actually a part of human nature.

Matter and its limitations are not part of God-established reality.

Sin is defined as a missing of the mark.

The belief of life in matter is sin.

All belief in a life apart from God is sinful.

Jesus' atonement doesn't provide people with forgiveness, but it gives us them the spiritual means to overcome sin.

If the practitioner can get someone to believe enough they will get well.

From Christian Science Sourcebook

p7-8 "Christian Science does not deify Jesus, a point that its severest critics have sometimes said separates it conclusively from traditional Christianity. Yet Jesus' actual role in the achievement of humanity's salvation is as important to its theology as for traditional theology. His life of obedience and sacrifice is understood as the means through which the reality of being for humankind has broken through in the midst of ordinary human experience. This true spiritual selfhood is identified as the eternal Christ, as distinct from Jesus, although uniquely and fully incarnated in him. His mission is viewed as opening up the possibility for all men and women to make actual their own spiritual union with God. He did this by proving practically that neither sin nor suffering is part of authentic spiritual selfhood, or Christ."

p76 "…humanity's final destiny is, as we see it, a complete mastery and laying aside of the whole limiting concept of life in matter. It is the demonstration of Life as God and of Life's individual expression as spiritual and eternal, not subject to birth, to passage through time, or to death."

p87 " For Christian Science, this spiritual reality is the Kingdom of God revealed through Jesus' life of obedience and sacrifice. … What other Christians do not share is Christian Science's conviction that God is absolutely not the author of the conditions of finitude – meaning material existence- which gives rise to suffering and disease. This may well be the most significant nonnegotiable difference between Christian Science and traditional Christian theology. Christian Scientists understand God as the sovereign creator, absolutely distinct from his creation. However, they see the finitude of God's creation not as his creative will but as the way creation appears within the habitual limits of human perception."

p96 "To the question 'What is the cardinal point of the difference in my metaphysical system?' Mrs. Eddy replies, 'This: that *by knowing the unreality of disease, sin, and death*, you demonstrate the allness of God.'"

p106 "We believe that Jesus' atonement is absolutely vital to the destruction of sin in our lives. But his atonement doesn't provide us with automatic forgiveness. Instead it gives us the spiritual means for grappling with and overcoming sin. When sin is destroyed through repentance and regeneration and through taking part in Christ's atonement, we experience forgiveness. And we begin to see that sin never really was a part of our actual nature."

p109 "death is something other that what it seems to be, that ultimately it's deceptive, even as the solidarity of matter has been called into question from the standpoint of twentieth- century quantum physics."

p147 " The purpose of turning to God for healing is therefore not merely to change the evidence before the physical sense but to heal the deeper alienation of human thought from God......When a Christian Scientist fails to demonstrate the healing power of God in a given situation, he does not question the goodness of God. Instead he asks himself where he needs to bring his own thinking and living into closer conformity with God's law."

p159 "It isn't a matter of asking God to fix something and then blindly having faith that He will…. It does not rest on a blind faith in the unknown but on an enlightened understanding of God as infinite, divine Mind, Spirit, Soul, Principle, Life, Truth, and Love. It recognizes God as acting through universal, immutable, spiritual law, an understanding of which constitutes the Science of Christianity."

p206 "It's one thing to believe that God occasionally intervenes supernaturally with a miraculous healing. It's another to see healing as a way of life – to believe – as Christian Scientists do, that healing is not a matter of miracles but of learning about and acting upon God's spiritual laws."

p208 " it would be hypocritical to call going back and forth between medicine and Christian Science 'normal' for Christian Scientists. This is because full reliance on spiritual means for healing is really the only kind of practice within the parameters of legitimate Christian Science. When church members, as sometimes happens, opt for medical treatment, they're not put out of the church."

Some Topics Addressed in *Science and Health with Key to the Scriptures*

(Quotations below are all from *Science and Health* and are noted by page and line number.)

Jesus

361:9-17 "The Christian who believes in the First Commandment is a monotheist. Thus he virtually unites with the Jew's belief in one God, and recognizes that Jesus Christ is not God, as Jesus himself declared, but is the Son of God. This declaration of Jesus, understood, conflicts not at all with another of his sayings: 'I and my Father are one,'- that is, one in quality, not in quantity. As a drop of water is one with the ocean, a ray of light one with the sun, even so God and man, Father and son, are one in being. The Scripture reads: 'For in Him we live, and move, and have our being.'"

42:15-29 "The resurrection of the great demonstrator of God's power was the proof of his final triumph over body and matter, and gave full evidence of divine Science,-evidence so important to mortals. The belief that man has existence or mind separate from God is a dying error. This error Jesus met with divine Science and proved its nothingness. … Let men think they had killed the body! Afterwards he would show it to them unchanged. This demonstrates that in Christian Science the true man is governed by God--by good, not evil--and is therefore not a mortal but an immortal. Jesus had taught his disciples the Science of this proof."

44:28-45:5 "His disciples believed Jesus to be dead while he was hidden in the sepulcher, whereas he was alive, demonstrating within the narrow tomb the power of Spirit to overrule mortal, material sense. There were rock-ribbed walls in the way, and a great stone must be rolled from the cave's mouth; but Jesus vanquished every material obstacle, overcame every law of matter, and stepped forth from his gloomy resting-place, crowned with the glory of a sublime success, an everlasting victory."

Pentecost

46:30-47:9 "His students then received the Holy Ghost. By this is meant, that by all they had witnessed and suffered, they were roused to an enlarged understanding of divine Science, even to the spiritual interpretation and discernment of Jesus' teachings and demonstrations, which gave them a faint conception of the Life which is God. They no longer measured man by material sense. After gaining the true idea of their glorified Master, they became better healers, leaning no longer on matter, but on the divine Principle of their work. The influx of light was sudden. It was sometimes an overwhelming power as on the Day of Pentecost."

Death

427:13-16 "Death is but another phase of the dream that existence can be material. Nothing can interfere with the harmony of being nor end the existence of man in Science."

Belief about illness and why drugs appear to work

155:3-14 "When the sick recover by the use of drugs, it is the law of a general belief, culminating in individual faith, which heals; and according to this faith will the effect be. Even when you take away the individual confidence in the drug, you have not yet divorced the drug from the general faith. The chemist, the botanist, the druggist, the doctor, and the nurse equip the medicine with their faith, and the beliefs which are in the majority rule. When the general belief endorses the inanimate drug as doing this or that, individual dissent or faith, unless it rests on Science, is but a belief held by a minority, and such a belief is governed by the majority."

177:31 -178:7 "In such cases a few persons believe the potion swallowed by the patient to be harmless, but the vast majority of mankind, though they know nothing of this particular case and this special person, believe the arsenic, the strychnine, or whatever the drug used, to be poisonous, for it is set down as a poison by mortal mind. Consequently, the result is controlled by the majority of opinions, not by the infinitesimal minority of opinions in the sick-chamber."

187:6-12 "Here you may see how so-called material sense creates its own forms of thought, gives them material names, and then worships and fears them. With pagan blindness, it attributes to some material god or medicine an ability beyond itself. The beliefs of the human mind rob and enslave it, and then impute this result to another illusive personification, named Satan."

369:14-22 "We never read that Luke or Paul made a reality of disease in order to discover some means of healing it. Jesus never asked if disease were acute or chronic, and he never recommended attention to laws of health, never gave drugs, never prayed to know if God were willing that a man should live. He understood man, whose Life is God, to be immortal, and knew that man has not two lives, one to be destroyed and the other to be made indestructible."

IV) Final thoughts - What is going on with all of these therapies?

"And Jesus said to him, 'Go; your faith has made you well.' Immediately he regained his sight and began following Him on the road." Mark 10:52 (NASB)

Science has a long way to go to determine how much of a treatment's success is simply due to the patient's belief in the efficacy of the treatment. This is true of traditional medicine, alternative medicine and prayer. We will consider two final topics – 1)the scientific mechanism underlying a therapy and 2)faith and the placebo effect.

Mechanisms are not always what they seem.

Just because a theory is popular does not mean that it is always correct. It is much easier to describe an event (I was healed!) than it is to truly explain why it happens (I was healed because my qi was balanced!). A therapy based upon a purported energy system may in fact work, but for altogether different reasons than the assumed mechanism.

For example acupuncture is becoming more accepted as a conventional therapy, but not because of the concepts proposed by energy medicine practitioners.

"Many of the conventional health professionals who practice acupuncture have dispensed with such concepts [yin and yang, etc.]. Acupuncture points are seen to correspond to physiological and anatomical features such as peripheral nerve junctions, and diagnosis is made in purely conventional terms. ... The effects of acupuncture, particularly on pain, are at least partially explicable within a conventional physiological model Acupuncture is known to stimulate A delta [i.e.- nerve] fibers entering the dorsal horn of the spinal cord. These mediate segmental inhibition of pain impulses carried in the slower, unmyelinated C fibers [other nerve fibers] and, through connections in the midbrain, enhance descending inhibition of C fiber pain impulses at other levels of the spinal cord. This helps explain why acupuncture needles in one part of the body can affect pain sensation in another region. Acupuncture is also known to stimulate release of endogenous opioids and other neurotransmitters such as serotonin. This is likely to be another mechanism for acupuncture's effect, such as in acute pain and in substance misuse." Vickers, A and Zollman, C., ABC of complementary medicine: Acupuncture British Medical Journal Vol. 319, 1999.

Taking out the scientific jargon this passage says that needle stimulation at one point can trigger a nerve that can send a signal to the brain which then sends signals back to turn off pain. In this process neurotransmitters (small molecules that transfer information from one nerve to another) can be released to alleviate pain. So the real mechanism may have nothing to do with qi – we just don't know.

The Placebo Effect

During World War II Dr. Henry Beecher was trying to treat wounded soldiers, but morphine was in short supply. He discovered that a significant amount of pain could be controlled with saline injections. He called this the **"placebo effect,"** which he later researched and found that up to 35% of a response to a medical treatment could be from the result of belief. This was one of the first instances in modern Western medicine that "the importance of belief reentered the web of health care." http://nccam.nih.gov/health/backgrounds/mindbody.htm

Whole books have been written about this phenomena such as Herbert Benson's Timeless Healing - The Power and Biology of Belief. Fireside (Simon & Schuster) 1997. Benson replaces the word "placebo" with "remembered wellness" because " it more accurately describes the brain mechanics involved [and] because the term 'placebo effect' has become pejorative in medical usage….an individual's belief empowers the placebo. The fact that the patient, caregiver, or both of them believe in the treatment contributes to better outcomes." p20-21

Benson describes "Three components of remembered wellness"

1. "Belief and expectancy on the part of the patient."

2. "Belief and expectancy on the part of the caregiver."

3. "Belief and expectancies generated by a relationship between the patient and the care giver" p32.

Many scientific studies have been done to test the placebo effect. Cavanna et. al. review several studies on neurological disorders and find that placebos can be administered and pain will be reduced. By some unknown mechanism real neurotransmitters are released that reduce pain, and the effects of the placebo can be blocked pharmacologically by giving the patient other drugs that block the effects of those neurotransmitters.

It has been demonstrated that symptoms of Parkinson's disease can be reduce with placebos. In certain studies 35% of depressed patients showed some improvement on placebo treatment. Imaging studies have shown that "placebo procedures raise expectations about future events and can trigger different neural pathways affecting not only pain perception, but also movement, mood and immunomodulation." Cavanna, A.E., Strigaro, G. and Monaco, F., Brain Mechanisms Underlying the Placebo Effect in Neurological Disorders Functional Neurology, 22(2) 89-94 2007.

V) CONCLUSION

We have a lot to learn about the nature of healing from both medical and theological perspectives. There is no pure "Christian" therapy in any of the many medical traditions. To compound the problem exactly why treatments appear to work may depend to a significant extent on what a patient believes. If a method of treatment is not consistent with a patient's belief system, it is not as likely to work, and is more likely to have unwanted effects. Prayerful consideration of treatment options can only help.

"At Lystra a man was sitting who had no strength in his feet, lame from his mother's womb, who had never walked. This man was listening to Paul as he spoke, who, when he had fixed his gaze on him and had seen that he had faith to be made well, said with a loud voice, 'Stand upright on your feet.' And he leaped up and began to walk". Acts 14:8-10 (NASB)

Notes

Notes

Chapter 13: The Healing River and Its Contributing Streams Part 1

Lesson Goals

1) To examine briefly specific denominations and streams in the Body of Christ and show their widespread contributions to the theology of healing.

2) To help bring clarity to some misleading theologies in certain streams specifically Word of Faith and Faith Cure Movements that I personally had to battle through.

3) To help guide through Catholic, Anglican and early Protestant doctrines and theologies concerning healing.

Introduction

1) **Leslie Weatherhead predicts Psychoneuroimmunology School in mid-1950's**

2) **MD's more open to healing than MDiv's**

3) **Two main sources for this unbelief in Theology**
   - Liberalism
   - Cessationsism

4) **The main reasons for the medical unbelief**
   - Enlightenment thinking
   - Closed naturalistic Newtonian World view

5) **Pursuit of Unity**
   - Unity in Diversity
   - Reduce Hostility between Ministers

6) **Two Things Happening at this Time**
   - New Age Movement
   - Church being reawakened to the Ministry of Healing

7) **Christianity has greatest emphasis on healing of all major Religions**
   - Biblical Record in Gospels and Acts indicate this emphasis
   - The Message of the Kingdom was central

     -Healing – central not peripheral

     -Deliverance – central not peripheral
   - History of Christianity also bears this statement out to be true (Ramsay McMullen, <u>Christianization of the Roman Empire</u>)

Key Insights

I) Anti-Nicene Church

A) 300 years of Healing and Deliverance Ministry

B) Apostles, Deacons, Evangelists, laypersons, priests and Bishops

II) Catholicism and Healing

A) Reliquial Healing

B) Healing through the Sacrament of the Eucharist

C) Healing in the sacrament of the Anointing of the Sick

D) Healing and the Holy People – too limited view – negative impact

E) Sickness and Suffering – negative implications

F) Authentication-evidential purpose of miracle – doctrine – negative implication

G) Moving from Warfare Worldview to Blueprint worldview (Augustine) – negative

H) Middle Ages changed meaning of the sacrament of Anointing of the Sick to "last rites" and only by Priest or Bishop

I) More biblical view of miracles than early Protestants had

J) Context today, needs to be more of the supernatural in the R.C. Church

K) Message would be rare from the average pulpit in Western Church or Northern Hemisphere

L) Impact upon liturgy

M) Pastoral impact

III) Historical Protestant Reformation Denominations and Healing

A) Historical Context and problem of authority – 2 problems

    (1) Evidential view of miracle of Catholicism

    (2) Enthusiasts of Ana Baptist

B) Response was the development of cessationism

C) Calvin not as cessationist as cessationists are today – exception for miracles to occur in new fields of evangelism where the gospel had never been preached, these miracles could be expected to continue until the Church was established in that culture.

D) Sovereign healings still possible, gifts of healing not

E) Today, modified- soft-core cessationist – problem doesn't establish strong faith

F) Kept Catholic understanding of sickness and suffering passages in Bible

G) Adopted evidential purpose of miracles and then made the Catholic miracles false miracles.

H) Also adopted the Blueprint worldview

I) Gifts ended not only for laity but clergy

J) Routine role of the Charismata

K) Impact upon liturgy

L)   Pastoral Impact

IV) Anglicanism and Healing

A)   1500's concerning quotes from the Book of Common Prayer

B)   1854 book <u>Visitatio Infirmorum</u>

C)   1928 passages removed, but tenor the same

D)   Evidence of the Blueprint worldview

E)   Language changed to positive for 2000 Book of Common Prayer

F)   Liberal Episcopalians another issue

G)   Father Morton Kelsey

H)   International Order of St. Luke the Physician

I)   Episcopal Priest, Mark Peason – Christian Healing - book

J)   Dr. Francis MacNutt's work within the Episcopal Church

K)   Large Charismatic Episcopal Churches and healing

L)   Liturgical impact

M)   Pastoral Impact

N)   What is positive about this position?

    (1)   God could still sovereignly heal

    (2)   Possible answer to intercessory or petitionary prayer for healing

O)   How the healing ministry was rediscovered within Protestantism

V)   The Faith Cure and the Word of Faith Streams

A) Similar but different

B) Faith Cure 1872 – Word of Faith 1970's

C) Most maligned for two reasons

1) #1 reason – extreme positions taken by some within the Word of Faith movement

2) *#2 reason* – Inaccurate historical research of D.R. McConnell, *A Different Gospel* – this book gets quoted and accepted by other scholars, but it is historically inaccurate – presuppositions also proven wrong due to this historical inaccuracy *(McIntyre, E. W. Kenyon and His Message of Faith: The True Story)*

D) My personal pilgrimage in regard to Word of Faith movement

1) Charismatic Movement in Seminary.
2) Impression: "The issue of your lifetime will be the Holy Spirit O.C.C.
3) Spillertown Baptist Church.
4) Exposure to Vineyard – antithesis of Word of Faith.
5) 13 years later – Rodney at Tulsa, Rhema.
6) 1,000 pastors would receive an "Impartation".
7) I had to repent of negative words against Word of Faith.
8) Influenced by inaccurate books – Hank, Dave, Paul, D.R. McConnell.
9) Divine set ups with divine appointment with Word of Faith people.
10) Mark Dupont's word in Berry, Ontario Summer 1994.
11) Acts 15 meeting with John Wimber.
12) 2004 meeting with Joe McIntyre and his book.
13) Learned about the true origins of Word of Faith – Faith Cure led by heroes of the Church.
14) Learned the true origins of Positive Confession – Methodism -Holiness.
15) George Peck and "Finished Work" influence on Gordon and Kenyon.
16) Faith Cure did not have emphasis on gifts of healing, healing evangelists, or anointing for healing – instead emphasis was upon promises of the Bible, and covenant relationship.
17) Faith Cure was very controversial in last quarter of 19th century.
18) Kenyon becomes major link between Faith Cure and Word of Faith.
19) F.F. Bosworth (*Christ the Healer*) brought Faith Cure teachings into Pentecostalism – though he was not a Pentecostal.
20) Unlike Pentecostalism, Faith Cure did not see God restoring the sign gifts to the church.
21) Neither the restoration of all the office gifts of Ephesians 4.
22) Faith Cure would have little impact on the liturgy of the service.
23) Faith Cure's impact upon pastor - importance .
24) Discovered Word of Faith had more scientific evidence for its benefit than other models – Dr. Benson "Cognitive Restructuring".
25) The conundrum of faith – disappointment or hopelessness.
26) Other models puts too much hope on the faith of the pray-er rather than the pray-ee whereas this model is often seen to put too much burden on the pray-ee rather than the pray-er.
27) The Scholarly apologia or theological treatises for Faith Healing of this period were:
    - *Stockmayer, nd (after 1867) Sickness and the Gospel. A.J. Gordon called Stockmayer* "the theologian of the doctrine of healing by faith".
    - *William Boardman, 1881. The Lord that Healeth Thee,* was a leader of the Keswick Holiness movement.
    - *J. Gordon, 1882. The Ministry of Healing: Miracles of Cure in All Ages.* Even his critic, B.B. Warfield, called Gordon's book, "ingenious", apologia and a "very persuasive "argument. *(Burgess, Dictionary)*
    - *R.L. Stanton, 1883. Gospel Parallelism: Illustrated in the Healing of Body and Soul.*
    - The leading apologia for healing was by R. Kelso Carter 1884. *The Atonement of Sin and Sickness: or A Full Salvation for Soul and Body.*

Notes

Notes

Chapter 14: The Healing River and Its Contributing Streams Part 2

Lesson Goals

1) Overview of the healing theologies of the Pentecostal Movements, Latter Rain revival and 3rd Wave Movement.
2) Emphasize the positive contributions that came from each movement and the effect each had upon the Body of Christ.
3) Bring to light the best doctrines in regard to healing from all major streams that represent truth.
4) Build a quality, comprehensive healing model representing all the major streams of the Body of Christ.

Introduction

This 2nd part of Healing Streams will focus more on the 20th century Church and where God is taking His Body in the third millennium. There have been several major moves of God in the past 100 years, and even though many denominations have been birthed from these moves, we don't want to summarily reject their theologies, but study them and find the truth in each of them. This chapter is an overview of the Pentecostal and 3rd Wave movements which heavily influenced my perspective of Christianity. Also, we will outline the best of all the movements in regards to healing to help create a comprehensive and effective model for prayer for healing.

Key Insights

I) The Classical Pentecostal Stream

A) Adopted the Faith Cure theology early on in its history

(1) The Evangelicals over-reacted and forsook anything that seemed to be associated with Pentecostalism, including healing – though it began as an Evangelical movement a quarter of a century before the Pentecostal movement began.

B) Not just personal faith, but also the faith of the evangelist plays a part

C) Early Pioneers:

(1) John Alexander Dowie
(2) John G. Lake
(3) Smith Wigglesworth
(4) Maria Woodworth-Etter
(5) Aimee Semple McPherson

D) Dr. Charles Price

(1) "Faith of God" vs "faith in God" emphasis

E) 1947 Latter Rain Movement renews power for healing.

(1) Emphasis upon equipping the saints for healing
(2) Why it ended? - They stopped focusing on equipping and began focusing on the offices.

F) 1948 Healing Revival

(1) Key Personalities
  a) William Branham
  b) Jack Coe

     c) A.A. Allen
     d) T.L. Osborn
     e) Oral Roberts
     f) Theme song: "all things are possible – only believe"
 2) Why it ended
     a) Lost ability to be awed – grieved the Holy Spirit
     b) Moral failure of evangelists

G) Emphasis of faith shifted from the promises and one's own faith to faith in the gift operative in the Healing Evangelist

H) Branham's double influence upon both the 1947 Latter Rain and the 1948 Healing Revival

(1) Missions of Latter Rain – Kenya "raising of the dead" - stop the funeral procession. Today thousands of churches exist as a result of this revival, after the raising of the dead.

(2) Key leaders of '48 healing revival inspired by Branham.

I) Changes in Liturgy effected by 1948 Healing Revival

(1) Special healing services

(2) Healing crusades with healing evangelists

(3) Pastors began to mimic for good and bad healing evangelists style

(4) Anointing with oil

(5) Handkerchiefs taken to the sick

(6) Stretcher services

(7) Restored emphasis on theology for healing that had existed in early Pentecostalism, but not as much on biblical teaching for healing as in the Faith Cure and the latter Word of Faith movements

J) Changes in liturgy effected by 1947 Latter Rain

(1) Teaching on healing

(2) Equipping the saints for healing

(3) Local church emphasis rather than the healing evangelist

(4) Prophetic presbyteries become important

(5) Emphasis on worship with the "heavenly choir"

(6) Gifts of healing could come to laity, not just the healing evangelist, pastor, and/or elders

K) Changes in liturgy effected by early Pentecostalism

(1) Anointing services

(2) Miracle services

(3) Handkerchiefs

(4) Healing homes – healing rooms

(5) Lake was an equipper

L) Impact of Latter Rain upon pastors

(1) Pastor sees key role of becoming an equipper through the local church

(2) Prophetic presbyteries

(3) Directive words from the presbytery

(4) Words had to be weighed by the pastor

(5) Pastors have high desire to move in gift of prophecy

(6) Strong belief in the grace of impartation or ability to impart

II)   The Equipping the Saints or Third Wave Stream

A) C. Peter Wagner – coined the term

B) John Wimber and Wagner key in birthing this movement
(1) John's background.
(2) Role of Fuller Theological Seminar.
(3) John's aversion to Pentecostal models and Pentecostal theology.
(4) Calling came through the study of the Bible rather than through fasting, impartation, or an angelic visitation. "pray or get out".
(5) 7 months before 1st healing.
(6) Honeycomb vision.
(7) Spreads around the world – emphasis not on the constituted gifts but the situational gifts of the Holy Spirit and "Everybody gets to pray" "Just do it" "Do the stuff".
(8) Not to be ashamed of the work of the Holy Spirit.
(9) Wimber's sons and daughters in the Vineyard.
(10) Wimber's sons and daughters outside the Vineyard
   • Che & Sue Ahn
   • John & Carol Arnott
   • Mike & Cherri Kaylor
   • Gary & Kathi Oates
   • Wes & Stacy Cambell
   • Rolland & Heidi Baker
   • Bill & Beni Johnson
   • Randy & DeAnne Clark

C) How does the equipping emphasis affect the liturgy of the service?
(1) Higher emphasis upon worship.
(2) "When my presence is in your midst in worship so is my power to heal."
(3) Spontaneous worship and new songs
(4) Words of Knowledge
(5) Prophecy
(6) Healing is an expectation at church.

D) How is the pastoral office affected?
(1) Pastor needs discernment
(2) Pastor needs to be well trained
(3) Pastor needs to have received an impartation
(4) Pastor is an equipper of the saints – a trainer
(5) Pastor is a drill sergeant rather than a paid chaplain

III) Developing an Integrative Model and Theology for Healing

A) The best from the Roman Catholic Church

    (1) Non-Cessationist Theology of Healing

    (2) Healing and the sacraments – Vatican II restored the Anointing for Healing sacrament to its original purpose of healing instead of preparing the soul to die.

    (3) Church Tradition – a positive side – the power of the Testimony

    (4) Low key models easier to apply

    (5) Post Vatican II emphasis on Holy Spirit and His Gifts

    (6) Inner Healing Model valued for removing blockages in physical healing

    (7) Insights from Dr. MacNutt

      a) Corrective understanding of "carrying our cross"; not bearing diseases.

      b) All Christians can pray for the sick, and move in the gifts, not just the most holy ones

      c) Deliverance is part of the healing ministry

      d) Authority – prayers of petition, intercession, and prayers of commands

B) The best from the Historical Protestant Reformation Denominations/ Churches

    (1) Miracles and other sign gifts can happen today when you are preaching to an un-reached people group. – John Calvin

    (2) God in His sovereignty can still heal today therefore prayer for healing by the congregation is appropriate, though the gift of healing is not given to individuals today. – This at least leaves room for congregational prayers for healing.

    (3) This tradition has the least positive contribution to make to the healing river.

C) The best from the Anglican Church

    (1) The 2000 Version of the Book of Common Prayer has removed the emphasis that illness is from God as a punishment and has a much more positive view of praying to God for healing from sickness.

    (2) The Anglican Church from the Southern Hemisphere is very conservative, believes in and practices healing and deliverance, and understands the Warfare worldview, though this would not characterize the Northern Hemisphere Anglican/Episcopal Churches.

    (3) Morton Kelsey's positive historical research proves healing has continued in every century.

    (4) Kelsey's re-mythologizing for the spiritually darkened thinkers influenced by Enlightenment philosophical presuppositions.

    (5) Positive contribution of the Order of St. Luke to healing ministry.

    (6) Mark Pearson's contribution through his book *Christian Healing*.

    (7) More open to Healing services in the local church than Lutheran and Reformed churches including Baptists who are predominantly Reformed in theology.

D) The best from the Faith Cure and Word of Faith Movements

    (1) The Faith Cure Movement originated within the Holiness Movement, both the Armenian/Methodist and the Reformed/Keswick movements – so naturally was rooted in mature leaders who believed in holiness.

    (2) Recaptured the biblical message of healing as central to the gospel and the work of Christ in the Atonement.

    (3) Scientific evidence on the power of "Positive Confession" called "cognitive restructuring" (Benson: Biology of Belief).

    (4) Understanding of the Noebo effect – opposite of placebo- Importance of avoiding negative confessions.

    (5) Strongest position regarding healing from Biblical perspective

(6) Provides strong basis to exercise faith – internal argument of the theology is consistent for strong faith

E) The best from the Pentecostal Denominations including Latter Rain and Healing Revival Denominations/Churches

(1) The Restoration of the Gift of Healing – additional basis for faith
(2) The Restoration of the Office of Healer – Healing Evangelists – additional basis for faith
(3) *Latter Rain – Equipping the saints emphasis – backdrop to restoration of the gifts and offices*
(4) *1948 Healing Revival – A basis to believe for greater things*
(5) *Within these denominations are where great healings and resurrections are occurring throughout the world*
(6) Builds on same theological basis as Faith Cure

F) The best from the Third Wave Denominations/Churches

(1) Builds on the Kingdom of God Now-Not yet
(2) Healing is through, though not in the Atonement
(3) Emphasis upon no hype or manipulation
(4) Emphasis upon not condemning the sick person
(5) Emphasis upon doing what we see the Father doing
(6) Emphasis upon not exaggerating the claims
(7) Emphasis on relationship between inner healing and physical healing

G) Building the Integrative Model for Healing

(1) Praying Petitions for Healing – petitionary model – theological basis – God's sovereignty
(2) Sacramental Praying for Healing – sacramental model – theological basis – Paul's understanding of discerning the body 1 Corinthians 11, also Acts 19 – prayer cloths of Paul
(3) Reliquial Healing – Power of the Testimony model & point of contact to release faith – Biblical model – Elisha's bones
(4) Inner healing prayers – Biblical Basis – Biblical Passages on Forgiveness
(5) Praying prayers of command – authority model – theological basis – Biblical Promises, Healing in the Atonement, Jesus' most frequent choice was commands.
(6) Confessing the Healing – Faith Cure and Word of Faith Model – theological basis – Scripture promises esp. 1 John 5:14-15 and Mark 11:23-26 - faith and forgiveness.
(7) Avoiding negative emotions and words (cognitive restructuring) Biblical Basis- Romans 12:1-2
(8) Prayers of command – based upon Kingdom now-not yet theology.
(9) A model that allows one to naturally move in the supernatural.
(10) A model that helps one understand how to recognize what the Father is doing.
(11) Yet, a model that encourages persevering and praying through.

Notes

Chapter 15: How to Receive and Give Words of Knowledge

Lesson Goals

1) To answer the question "What is a word of knowledge?"
2) To learn how to minister words of knowledge for healing.
3) To learn how to recognize when we are receiving words of knowledge, that is, how they may come to us or in what form we may receive them.
4) To examine some practical insights for growing in the use of words of knowledge for healing.
5) TO BE ACTIVATED IN WORDS OF KNOWLEDGE FOR HEALING!

Introduction

> **1 Corinthians 12:1,7-8**
> ¹Now concerning spiritual *gifts,* brethren, I do not want you to be unaware....⁷But to each one is given the manifestation of the Spirit for the common good. ⁸For to one is given the word of wisdom through the Spirit, and to another the word of knowledge according to the same Spirit; *(NASB95)*

Our Heavenly Father, after the resurrection of Jesus Christ, sent to His children the person of the Holy Spirit with all of His fruit and gifts made available to us. In 1 Corinthians 12:7, Paul wrote that the manifestation of the Spirit is given for the **common good**.

In this lesson we want to look at receiving **words of knowledge** for the release of healing. Notice this is an **activation clinic** session. At the end of the session, you will be given the opportunity to step out in faith to receive a word of knowledge for healing. This will be followed by the opportunity to then pray for the individual that has the condition described in the word of knowledge you received. In your ministry to that person, you will use the Five-Step Prayer Model discussed in the previous lesson.

Key Insights

I) What is a Word of Knowledge?

> **1 Corinthians 2:12-13**
> ¹²Now we have received, not the spirit of the world, but the Spirit who is from God, that we might know the things that have been freely given to us by God. ¹³These things we also speak, not in words which man's wisdom teaches but which the Holy Spirit teaches... *(NKJV)*

Simply, **a word of knowledge** is a supernatural revelation of information received through the Holy Spirit. It is knowledge received apart from natural analysis or human means. In this lesson we are focusing on Words of Knowledge for Healing.

II) Recognizing and Receiving A Word of Knowledge for Healing

A) How Does God Give A Word of Knowledge for Healing?

God gives His revelations in different ways, and that is true of words of knowledge for healing as well as for other kinds of revelation. Some of the more common ways He gives words of knowledge for healing are:

1. **Feel It**
2. **See It**

3. **Read It**
4. **Think It**
5. **Say It**
6. **Dream It**
7. **Experience It**

Let's now look at each of these in detail.

B) Examining Seven Common Ways to Receive

1) *Feel It*

You may have
- a sharp pain in some part of your body.
- a throbbing sensation.
- some other sensation.
- a strong emotion such as fear or panic.

Be careful that your feeling is not caused by a condition in your own body. For instance, if you often have pain in your left ear, you would not give that as a word of knowledge even if you get that pain during a meeting.

2) *See It*

You may get a mental picture, such as
- a body part: perhaps a heart, a foot, an eye, a head.
- a person with a certain condition such as a limp.
- a person carefully holding his arm.
- a crutch, eye-glasses, a person walking with a cane.
- a water bottle, a barbed wire fence, an auto accident.

3) *Read It*

You may see in your mind:
- a person with a word written across his front or back, or over his head.
- a word written on a wall or on a carpet.
- something like a newspaper headline, or a banner.

4) *Think It*

You may sense in your mind that someone has a particular condition, or that the Holy Spirit has spoken the word to you. It is a mental impression.

5) *Say It*

While talking or praying or standing with someone, unpremeditated words may tumble out of your mouth relating to a physical condition you were not aware of.

6) *Dream It*

While sleeping, you may have a vivid dream in which:
- you have a new health problem.
- you see someone with a health problem.
- you hear someone talking about a health problem.
- you see an event acted out before you like a movie, such as a hospital scene or an accident.

7) *Experience It*

Similar to dreaming it, you may have a vivid vision while awake. It may be so strong that you are actually a part of what is happening, not just an observer.

Sometimes these categories blend together. Is it a mental picture or a vision? Vision could be likened to a "3D Technicolor movie" - something given by the Holy Spirit that is beyond a mental picture in intensity and vividness.

III) Ministering A Word of Knowledge for Healing

A) The Holy Spirit Gives a Word of Knowledge for a Specific Need

The Holy Spirit often gives a revelatory word of knowledge concerning the need of a person (or persons) for healing. This is an indication that God wishes to heal the person or those who have the condition revealed in the word of knowledge, and <u>usually</u> that He wishes to heal <u>at the time the word is given</u>.

When understood in this way, a word of knowledge <u>builds faith in the person who needs the healing</u>, and also <u>in the person who received the word of knowledge</u>. Accordingly, the person who receives the word:
- Should usually speak it out at that time or at the next appropriate time.
- Should see if it applies to someone present, and if so, offer to pray at once for that person's healing.

B) The Context for Receiving a Word of Knowledge

(1) *You may receive a word of knowledge any time or anywhere.*

You might get a word during a prayer meeting, a cell group meeting, walking past someone in church or in the supermarket, or while washing dishes at home.

(2) *You may or may not know for whom the revelation has been given.*

Most often, the word of knowledge is given for someone present. However, it may not be for someone present, but for a person whom someone present knows about. Or it can be for someone you will see in the near future.

C) Specificity in Expressing a Word of Knowledge for Healing and the Effect on Faith

<u>The more specific the word of knowledge is, the more faith it builds in the people involved</u>. If the word is received through feeling a pain, it is helpful if the kind of pain and its exact location is stated.

For example, it is better to say, "A shooting pain on the left side of the neck just below the ear", or to point to the exact location, than to say merely, "A pain in the neck," or, "Does someone's neck hurt?"

D) Expressing a Word of Knowledge Only as Received

The person receiving the word should be careful not to change it, and not to add to it. When shared it should not be exaggerated, nor any detail left out of that seems unimportant. Changes or additions cause confusion.

Personal Illustration: Randy: the man and the <u>green</u> hose.
I once had a mental picture of someone being injured by tripping over a green hose. The only green hoses I had seen were garden hoses. So I said I had a picture of a person injured by tripping over a green *garden* hose. There was a man in the meeting who had been injured by tripping over a green *pressure* hose at work. He did not respond to my word at first, because the hose he tripped on wasn't a *garden* hose. He would have responded more quickly if I had not assumed that the green hose was a garden hose and had given it just as I had seen it.

E) How to Deliver a Word of Knowledge for Healing

(1) *It is generally wise to be tentative in speaking out the word you have received.*

For example, you might say, "Does anyone have a sharp pain in his left elbow just now?" If no one responds, don't be concerned. If someone responds you could say, "Well, I just had a sharp pain in my left elbow, which may be a word of knowledge indicating that God would like to heal you now. Since you have that condition, would you like for me (or us) to pray for you now?"

(2) *If the person is open to receiving prayer, pray for him.*

If he wants prayer later, pray for him later. If he doesn't want prayer due to embarrassment, lovingly encourage him to receive. <u>But if he refuses, don't pressure him in any way to receive prayer.</u>

IV) Practical Insights for Growing in the Use of a Word of Knowledge for Healing

A) A word of knowledge may come quickly.

Words of knowledge may come flitting through your mind more like a bird or dancing butterfly than like a stationary billboard.

B) A word of knowledge may be rather vague, tempting you to screen it out or to ignore it.

Practice "tuning in" to these revelations and speaking them out. If you are tentative and humble, not arrogant or presumptuous, no one will be offended if you seem to have heard amiss.

C) Resist the thought that a word you have received is not important, or that it is "just you".

Remember, it builds faith in the <u>other person</u> to know that God has revealed that person's condition to you. What seems like a <u>vague</u> impression <u>to you</u> may be a <u>shout</u> to <u>the other person</u>! However, don't be presumptuous. Don't say, "God just told me you have an earache." Instead, say, "Does your left ear ever bother you? I have an impression of a problem in a left ear. Does this mean anything to you?"

D) Unpretentious honesty is the best policy!

It's perfectly okay:
- to admit that you're nervous.
- to say that you have only a vague impression.
- to say that you have never had a word for someone before.
- to say that praying for sick people is new to you.

E) Don't let fear rob you and the person who might have been healed.

Someone has said that "faith" is spelled "r-i-s-k". Be patient, but step out! Be humble, but ***step out***! Be tentative, but STEP OUT! God is giving you words of knowledge because He wants you to use them! He wants you to use them *wisely* and *prudently* and *humbly*, but He DOES want you to use them!

Activation

We now get to the fun part! Again, if you have NEVER received a word of knowledge, don't be afraid! Step out on the FAITHFULNESS of God and into the REVELATION of the Holy Spirit.

Remember:
- **Gifts are given to us in the "Finished Work of Jesus Christ" in His atonement.**
- **Gifts are received by asking.**
- **Gifts are drawn to those who hunger and thirst for spiritual things.**
- **Gifts are received through faith, like everything else in the Kingdom**
-

My Personal History
I had been in the ministry 14 years without ever recognizing a word of knowledge.

I had both a B.S. degree in Religious Studies and a Master of Divinity degree from the School of Theology, but had no understanding of how to move in the gift of word of knowledge.

The very week I was told five ways you could have a word of knowledge I began having them.

One week later I taught on words of knowledge for the first time in my life. That very evening a woman had a word that led to a healing!

Ever since then every time I have taught on this subject, and given God the opportunity, there has always been someone who received their first words of knowledge. I have taught this teaching hundreds of times.

Today we shall see God be faithful once again, and at least 10% of this crowd who have never had a word of knowledge will have their first word of knowledge. I am going to pray and wait for 2 minutes during which time some of you who have never had a word of knowledge will have your first word of knowledge. I have never taught this when God didn't give people words of knowledge.

On one of our first trips to Brazil, one-half of the team on that bus had NEVER had a word of knowledge or seen anyone healed. I told them that before 2 days was over they would all have a word of knowledge and pray for someone who would be healed. It happened and has continued to happen!

SO, GET READY TO BE ACTIVATED!

Notes

Chapter 16: My Personal Experience of Healing - Part 2

Lesson Goals

1.) To gain a better understanding of the various major streams of healing within Christianity.
2.) To challenge the presuppositions of Liberalism, Cessationism, Dispensationalism, and by informing people, schooled in these systems, of the continuation of miraculous power for healing in our day.
3.) To encourage faith by "the power of the testimony" for healing.
4.) To challenge the technological/tool emphasis for valid testing of the Scientific Method; the limits of science.
5.) To emphasize the uniqueness of the human being to experience the spiritual realm, that humans are the best "tool" for perceiving the reality of the spiritual realm.

Introduction

This lesson is a continuation of the previous chapter on Personal Experiences Part 1. I believe that there are limitations to the scientific method. There are things that are real, are experienced, repeatable (but not consistent), that science hasn't been able to verify primarily because the scientific community has not yet developed the tools to quantify and verify the existence of such realities. For example there was radiation before there was a Geiger counter to prove it. The law of aerodynamics existed before a plane was built. There were germs before we had a microscope to see them.

I believe the human being has the ability to discern and experience realities that our technological machines have not yet been developed to quantify or verify. But, to deny the human experience of these realities, merely because we don't presently understand the yet-to-be-discovered laws that govern them, is intellectual dishonesty. We must now allow the "dogma" of science to threaten the discovery of truth in the same way that the "dogma" of religion stood in the way of scientific discovery.

Key Insights

I) Neurological damage

A) Charlie, spinal damage, healed at Vineyard – fireball hit him sovereignly.

B) Man who couldn't lift feet from floor – Join Villa, Brazil 2002-03.

C) Anne Harrison--last stages of Parkinson's (afflicting spirit theory or bitterroot judgment theory, mother was same age 1995-96).

D) Women healed of Multiple Sclerosis (2007) Las Vegas and Castle Rock, CO.

E) Pastor healed of Parkinson's (2007) Denver.

F) Schizophrenia and severe obsessive compulsive disorder – Julie in Tucson, Arizona meeting September 2007.

G) Tucson, Arizona same night as Julie's healing, another woman with Schizoaffective Disorder and her adult son who was bi-polar healed.

II) Hydrocephalic/Spina Bifida

A) Tammy Ferguson, also had seizures – Marion Illinois healed 1984

B) Man at Harrisburg, PA healing school – small child's vision or dream healed through prayers of children, had never walked without calipers - healed 2004

III) Rare diseases

A) Kat McNallie— 1996 diagnosed with a rare auto-immune disorder called Takayasu's Arteritis (TA) for which there is no cure. Her life expectancy at that time was 3-5 years.

   (1) Had chemotherapy with no success. She was healed of TA at Randy Clark renewal meeting in NY in 2002.

   (2) Was told impossible to have children, but gave birth in 2005. She bled internally however a day later before anyone realized it, and 7 blood transfusions and 2 fresh frozen plasma transfusions later, she had emergency surgery to remove the 7 lb hematoma that had developed in her stomach.

   (3) Due to the many transfusions, she contracted TA again and underwent chemotherapy again.

   (4) Randy prayed for her again and she was healed of TA again!!

   (5) Severe Blood clotting throughout legs and pelvis area – healed at Harrisburg healing school - 2004.

IV) Paraplegics

A) 25 yr. old man in Manaus, Brazil bullet wound severed spinal cord.

B) Man 5 yr. from car accident Belem, Brazil Quadrangular Church Crusade.

V) Resurrections

A) Rego's story

B) Johnny's story

C) Mr. & Mrs. Donweckie's stories

D) Surprise Sithole story

E) Guitar player's son in Ohio Valley (Indiana)

F) Black haired grandma goes on our trips – grandson drowned (USA) Nancy

G) Omar Cabrera's story - drowned minister friend's wife

H) Omar Jr.'s brother

I) Bill's latest story (2008)

J) Brazil in Randy's meeting (2008)

Chapter 17: Psychological Schools of Thought and Their Relationship to Healing

Lesson Goals

1) Introduce the reader to early modern medicine as it sought to treat hysteria and general medical problems
2) Gain a brief overview of five schools of psychology that developed in the twentieth century
3) Look at some of the streams of inner healing, and see how they might be helpful through case studies

Introduction

In this section we will look at the modern history of medical and psychological interventions for emotional healing. If every good and perfect gift comes down from above, from the Father of lights, then even secular psychotherapies and medical care can be seen as gifts from God. It turns out ministries of inner healing have some relationship to various schools of psychology, so it is helpful to have some understanding of their history and theory.

Key Insights

I) One of the first modern physicians to treat hysteria along with his general patients was Dr. Thomas Sydenham

II) Thomas Sydenham (1624-1689), a physician of London, was called the Hippocrates of modern medicine.

He was attributed with recommending Peru bark (quinine) for malaria, for treating severe pain with laudanum (opium), for writing extensive histories of various fevers, including scarlatina, and was known for describing the tremor, Sydenham's chorea, that scarlatina and rheumatic fever produced. He also studied hysteria extensively, and was a compassionate observer who followed the Hippocratic dictum, "First, do no harm." The following is his quote:

> "Whoever takes up medicine should seriously consider the following points: firstly, that he must one day render to the Supreme Judge an account of the lives of those sick men who have been entrusted to his care. Secondly, that such skill and science as, by the blessing of Almighty God, he has attained, are to be specially directed toward the honour of his Maker, and the welfare of his fellow-creatures; since it is a base thing for the great gifts of Heaven to become the servants of avarice and ambition. Thirdly, he must remember that it is no mean or ignoble animal that he deals with. We may ascertain the worth of the human race, since for its sake God's Only-begotten Son became man, and thereby ennobled the nature that he took upon him. Lastly, he must remember that he himself hath no exemption from the common lot, but that he is bound by the same laws of mortality and liable to the same ailments and afflictions with his fellows. For these and like reasons let him strive to render aid to the distressed with the greater care, with the kindlier spirit, and with the stronger fellow-feeling."

Medical Observations, 1st edition, Preface.
Translated by R. G. Latham in Works, Volume 1.

III) Above we see how a godly physician or therapist will honor the one in their charge as a child of God.

Below is an excerpt from Ecclesiasticus, one of the Wisdom books, written around 180 B.C. It shows that the people had a way of honoring their doctors:

> **Ecclesiasticus 38: 1-5**
>
> Honor the doctor for his services, for the Lord created him; His skill comes from the Most High, and he is rewarded by kings. The doctor's knowledge gives him high standing, And wins him the admiration of the great. The Lord has created medicines from the earth, And a sensible man will not disparage them. (The New English Bible)

IV) Another early researcher in hysteria was a French physician, Dr. Jean Martin Charcot.

He took careful case histories of hysteria and noticed that they were usually traced to early traumatic memories. The young physician, Dr. Sigmund Freud came to study with him in Paris briefly, during his training years. Later Freud came to conclude that early sexual fantasies and the conflict about them was the primary source of hysteria, rather than early traumas that might actually include sexual abuse. This idea that the trauma must be a fantasy persisted in Freudian psychology for quite a while, and reinforced the deceptions in dysfunctional families: "Nothing really happened," or "If something happened, it was probably your fault, and it is better not to talk about it." We might wonder how Freud and early psychiatrists could do such a thing, but there is a natural tendency to hope that the darker things of human behavior did not happen, or at least a wish to look away.

A) There are many churches and pastors who say we do not need to look at the past. They will say that Paul encouraged us to forget the past:

> **Philippians 3:13-14**
>
> Brethren, I do not count myself to have apprehended; but one thing I do, forgetting those things which are behind and reaching forward to those things which are ahead, I press toward the goal for the prize of the upward call of God in Christ Jesus. (NKJV)

B) But in the context of these verses Paul is explaining how he previously would boast in His Hebrew heritage and training, as a Pharisee of the Pharisees. His identity now as a believer is completely in Christ and in the power of His resurrection, and he no longer looks back to the old ways of self-righteousness.

C) This is much different from looking for old wounds that may be partially hidden but still exert power over a believer through strongholds in the spiritual realm.

V) Freudian School

The school of psychoanalytic psychotherapies began with Dr. Sigmund Freud, (1856-1939) a Viennese neurologist who became a psychiatrist. In his first years of developing his theories, he would meet with other physicians in his office every Wednesday night. Two of these early colleagues later developed their own schools, Alfred Adler and Carl Jung. But Freud would go on to develop theories that drives and fantasies came from a structure of the mind called the id, and were modified by the superego and the ego which eventually balanced these drives and conflicts through a series of defense mechanisms. He felt much could be learned from the subconscious mind of the patient, though he was not the first to use that term. To understand what was happening in the subconscious mind, he would instruct his analysand to state whatever was on his or her mind, to "free-associate." This was a novel concept that has imbedded within it a lack of judgmental attitude and an unconditional acceptance of his patient, not unlike the unconditional love of the Bible. Since Christianity had stepped back from healing the whole person, including the mind, Freudian psychology stepped into the void. Two good books for Christians are *Freud vs. God: How Psychiatry Lost Its Soul and Christianity Lost Its Mind,* by Dan Blazer, M.D., and *The Question of God: C.S. Lewis and Sigmund Freud Debate God, Sex, and the Meaning of Life,* by Armand Nicholi, M.D.

VI) Adlerian School.

This school is also known as individual psychology. Alfred Adler (1870-1937) was a practicing physician in Vienna when Freud invited him to his Wednesday night discussion group. When it later developed into the Psychoanalytic Society he was one of its first presidents, in 1908. But by 1910 he broke from Freud because they both realized his ideas were much different. He felt individuals were primarily motivated by a need to become complete or self-empowered, not primarily by instincts or drives. He believed that by encouragement, people could learn to make healthy choices for their own goals and for the good of their family or group. Terms like self-defeating behavior, power struggle and the inferiority complex came from individual psychology. He did focus on normal development and functioning, not on mental illness. In a positive way he taught that people could learn to make better choices, giving rise to modern psychotherapies like Rational Emotive Therapy (Albert Ellis) and Cognitive Therapy (Aaron Beck). He described the importance of birth order in the family constellation, and he believed in teaching parenting skills at the child guidance clinics he founded. He was born Jewish but later converted to Christianity. Adler could be seen as the "son of encouragement," the Barnabas of psychological teachers. When you read Christian authors like Kevin Leman, *Making Children Mind Without Losing Yours,* you are reading a lot of Adler's ideas.

> **Philippians 2:4**
>
> Let each of you look out not only for his own interests, but also for the interests of others. (NKJV)

VII) Jungian School.

Carl Gustav Jung (1875-1961) was another psychiatrist in Freud's early circle, who came from Switzerland to work for a time in Vienna. Like Adler, he eventually developed his own ideas on understanding the mind of man, and he too would leave Freud completely, by 1914. Jung was the son of a Lutheran pastor, and from the beginning in psychoanalysis he looked for religious or spiritual symbols in the thoughts and dreams of his patients. He felt these symbols were drawn from the collective unconscious and the recurring patterns were from ancient archetypes. He studied Western and Eastern religions and some of his ideas, such as the anima and animus in the soul, have roots in the dualism of Buddhism or Eastern mysticism. But he felt the most important drive in the second half of life was the drive to find meaning in one's faith, to know who we are in relation to God. To affirm the world of the spirit, apart from body and mind, was quite a departure from the origins of psychoanalysis, something Freud could not recommend. He felt dream interpretation was even more important than Freud did. Christian ministries that interpret dreams, like Streams Ministries International, can look back to some of the foundational work done by Jung. But when interpreting the influence of dreams and spiritual forces in a person's life, the discernment of a committed Christian would help a Jungian analysis.

> **I John 4:1-2**
>
> Beloved, do not believe every spirit, but test the spirits, whether they are of God; because many false prophets have gone out into the world. By this you know the Spirit of God: Every Spirit that confesses that Jesus Christ has come in the flesh is of God. (NKJV)

VIII) Behavioral School.

This school is most associated with B. F. Skinner (1904-1990). More than other schools, there is emphasis on the biologic or animal nature of man. Behavior is shaped or trained according to patterns the brain perceives from experience and seeking reward, which may be neurochemical. Terms like reinforcement and operant conditioning came from his work. Today many anxiety disorders, like panic disorder with agoraphobia, seem to respond best to behavioral treatments like graded exposure to the stimulus (crowds of people) until the startle response is reduced. In some ways the approach of modern medicine and psychiatry to reach first for pharmacologic treatment of mental distress is similar to the biologic model of behaviorism. This diminishes the value of the mind or psyche, and ignores the importance of the spirit entirely. We need to be careful of exalting the mind. As Bill Johnson says, "The mind is a good follower but a poor leader."

> **Romans 8:14**
>
> For as many as are led by the Spirit of God, these are the sons of God. (NKJV)

IX) Attachment Theory

This school is associated with John Bowlby (1907-1990) who studied patterns of infant attachment to their mothers. His early work was augmented by the work of Mary Ainsworth who also studied patterns of maternal infant attachment. She would say she observed three general patterns of attachment: secure attachment, anxious-ambivalent attachment, and anxious-avoidant attachment. Earlier than both of these was research on severe maternal deprivation by Rene Spitz when he studied the effects of deprivation on orphans who were displaced from London foundling homes during World War II. They not only look depressed, they looked malnourished from failure to thrive, and he called this anaclitic depression. Christian teachers in recent years have re-emphasized being immersed in the Father's love as part of the healing process.

> **John 14:18**
>
> I will not leave you orphans; I will come to you. (NKJV)

X) Heidi Baker and others would call this healing the orphan spirit.

Combining attachment theory with understanding our own attachment to the Lord gave a group of therapists the Life Model, described by Friesen, Wilder and others in a booklet *Living From the Heart Jesus Gave You.* They speak of type A traumas (neglect) and type B traumas (abuse) and their healing when the believer returns to the joy of the Lord's Presence, and learns to carry His Presence into every situation.

> **Psalm 16:11**
>
> You will show me the path of life; in Your Presence is fullness of joy; at Your right hand are pleasures forevermore.

XI) Streams of Inner Healing.

Inner healing is a generic term for various models of prayer or prayer counsel for healing of emotional distress. For the most part, inner healing models do not follow a medical model nor do they need to be associated with any particular school of psychology or psychotherapy. It may be just as well that the ministry of healing stays separate from medical and psychotherapy models, to retain their own identity, their unique effectiveness, and to avoid malpractice litigation when they do not claim to be a licensed therapy. In practice, a Christian psychiatrist or psychologist will often have case examples in which people have been helped by medical interventions to help the body heal, psychotherapies to help the mind heal, and inner healing prayer to help body, soul, and spirit be healed and delivered out of spiritual distress.

Listed below are some of the well known schools of inner healing and deliverance. It is beyond the scope of this course to teach these models, but by consulting their websites and signing up for their courses you can learn the basics then learn how to use their techniques in prayer for inner healing:

Christian Healing Ministries, Francis and Judith MacNutt,   www.christianhealingmin.org

Elijah House Ministries, John and Paula Sandford,   www.elijahhouse.org

Restoring The Foundations Ministry, Chester and Betsy Kylstra   www.healinghouse.org

Theophostic Ministry, Ed Smith,   www.theophostic.com

Sozo Ministry,   Bethel Church, Redding, California   www.ibethel.org
See also a new book at Global Awakening resource table, Freedom Tools, by Andy Reese, on Sozo

Cleansing Stream Ministries, Chris Hayward   www.cleansingstream.org

Streams Ministries International, John Paul Jackson   www.streamsministries.com

Freedom in Christ Ministries, Neil Anderson   www.ficm.org

XII) One final exercise will be to look at case studies of individuals who were beset with fear and with anger and see how ministry from various streams of inner healing bring wholeness and deliverance.

Psalm 46: 4-5

There is a river whose streams shall make glad the city of God, the holy place of the tabernacle of the Most High. God is in the midst of her, she shall not be moved; God shall help her, just at the break of dawn. (NKJV)

Notes

Chapter 18: Areas Where More Understanding is Needed

This session will a be panel discussion with speakers addressing questions from the participants.

Notes

Notes

Chapter 19: Where Do We Go from Here?

I) Future Symposia – Building Bridges between the Medical and Christian healing Communities

II) Developing a trademarked training course with various levels of certification for healing.

    A)   That is open to anyone who loves people. Anyone could gain from the training and see healing if they understand the principles that underlie the causes of some illness and the spiritual principles that can effect healing.

III) Global Awakening Media Projects

    A)   Development of training videos to introduce the Christian healing perspective to the medical community

    B)   Development of WLI Online training and online training with other universities

    C)   Development of 4-part video series for use in hospitals

    D)   Development of video shows for possible use on Discovery Channel, Discovery Health and Miracle Net, India

    E)   Development of a History of Healing program for the HistoryChannel

    F)   Creating new "Christian reality" programming for secular networks

    G)   Raising and equipping a media army through two-day training camps for still and video production

IV) Developing a curriculum to be offered online to colleges and universities called- Theopathic Care and Curing.

V) Schools of Healing and Impartation

    A) Revival Phenomena and Healing

    B) Healing, Deliverance and Disbelief

    C) Spiritual and Medical Perspectives

VI) Using the Apostolic Resource Center as a resource for developing stronger healing perspectives, an apostolic framework for church communities and prophetic/supernatural revelation and activation.

VII) Other Global Awakening projects. including international missions out reach, marketplace transformation, crisis aid and intervention.

Notes

Chapter 20: Challenges Facing the Church in the 3rd Millenium

Lesson Goals

1) One of the major challenges facing the church in the 3rd millennium is to recapture the faith of the early Church in the words of Jesus and the Apostles as recorded in Scripture.
2) In order to do this, various doctrinal systems must be seen to fall short of what the Bible actually teaches: Dispensationalism, Cessationism, Liberalism.
3) There is a lack of discernment within the Church regarding heretical interpretations of the Christian doctrine. i.e. New-Age threats similar to the Gnostic heresy of the first couple of centuries.
4) To create a hunger and a faith to experience all that Jesus promised us.

Introduction

The greatest challenge I have when I read the Bible is not the passages that are hard to understand, but those that are very clear, easy to understand. It can be hard to have sufficient faith to step into the reality of experience in which the Bible invites us. Rather than enter into the experience the Bible invites us, or Jesus, Paul, etc…, we have developed theological constructs which allow us not to expect to experience these realities. These are interpretations of the Bible that actually undermine the very words of Jesus. Just as the Church has always had to deal with heresy in its history, it still must do so today. One of the most threatening today is the heresy of a new Gnosticism known as the New Age. I believe its success has, in part, been made possible by the Church having developed these theologies or systems of thought that greatly lessened the supernatural dimension of its life and experience.

Key Insights

I) The Bible and Hermeneutical Problems

A) We have a serious problem with the Bible. It isn't with the obscure passages that are hard to discern where our most serious problems lie, but with the very clear, forthright, easily understandable passages. The problem is that much of the Church doesn't believe these words are true for us today. Passages such as follow:

John 14:12-14

[12]I tell you the truth, <u>anyone</u> who has faith in me will do what I have been doing. He will do even greater things than these, because I am going to the Father. [13]And I will do whatever you ask in my name, so that the Son may bring glory to the Father. [14]You may ask me for anything in my name, and I will do it. (NIV emphasis added)

John 15:7-8

[7]If you remain in me and my words remain in you, ask whatever you wish, and it will be given you. [8]This is to my Father's glory, that you bear much fruit, showing yourselves to be my disciples.

Mark 16:17

[17]And these signs will accompany those who believe: In my name they will drive out demons; they will speak in new tongues; they will pick up snakes with their hands; and when they drink deadly poison, it will not hurt

them at all; they will place their hands on sick people, and they will get well.

James 5:14-16

[14]Is any one of you sick? He should call the elders of the church to pray over him and anoint him with oil in the name of the Lord. [15]And the prayer offered in faith will make the sick person well; the Lord will raise him up. If he has sinned he will be forgiven. [16]Therefore, confess your sins to each other and pray for each other so that you may be healed. The prayer of a righteous man is powerful and effective.

Mark 11:22-24

[22]"Have faith in God", Jesus answered. [23]"I tell you the truth, if anyone says to this mountain, 'Go, throw yourself into the sea,' and does not doubt in his heart but believes that what he says will happen, it will be done for him. [24]Therefore I tell you, whatever you ask for in prayer, believe that you have received it, and it will be yours."

Matthew 17:19-21

[19]Then the disciples came to Jesus in private and asked, "Why couldn't we drive it out?" [20]He replied, "Because you have so little faith. I tell you the truth, if you have faith as small as a mustard seed, you can say to this mountain, 'Move from here to there' and it will move. Nothing will be impossible for you."

Luke 17:5-6

[5]The apostles said to the Lord, "Increase our faith!" [6]He replied, "If you have faith as small as a mustard seed, you can say to this mulberry tree, 'Be uprooted and planted in the sea,' and it will obey you."

　　•(The above three references to the power of faith are at different times and contexts and do not appear to be parallels. But different times Jesus made these statements indicating what a major theme it was to him.)

Matthew 7:7-8

[7]Ask and it will be given to you; seek and you will find; knock and the door will be opened to you. [8]For everyone who asks receives; he who seeks finds; and to him who knocks, the door will be opened.

Matthew 18:19-20

[19]Again, I tell you that if two of you on earth agree about anything you ask for, it will be done for you by my Father in heaven. [20]For where two or three come together in my name, there am I with them.

Luke 11:9-10

[19]So I say to you: Ask and it will be given to you; seek and you will find; knock and the door will be opened to you. [10]For everyone who asks receives; he who seeks finds; and to him who knocks, the door will be opened.

Luke 10:1, 9, 17

[1]After this the Lord appointed seventy-two others and sent them two by two ahead of him to every town and

place where he was about to go. . . . [9]Heal the sick who are there and tell them, "The kingdom of God is near you." . . . [17]The seventy-two returned with joy and said, "Lord, even the demons submit to us in your name."

Matthew 10:1, 7-8a

[1]He called his twelve disciples to him and gave them authority to drive out evil spirits and to heal every disease and sickness. . . . [7]As you go preach this message: "The kingdom of heaven is near." [8]Heal the sick, raise the dead, cleanse those who have leprosy, drive out demons.

Mark 6:7, 12-13

[7]Calling the Twelve to him, he sent them out two by two and gave them authority over evil spirits. . . . [12]They went out and preached that people should repent. [13]They drove out many demons and anointed many sick people with oil and healed them.

Matthew 28:19-20

[19]Then Jesus came to them and said, "All authority in heaven and on earth has been give to me. [19]Therefore go and make disciples of all nations, baptizing them in the name of the Father and of the son and of t he Holy Spirit, [20]and teaching them to obey everything I have commanded you. And surely I am with you always, to the very end of the age."

Acts 6:8

[8]Now Stephen, a man full of God's grace and power, did great wonders and miraculous signs among the people. (*He was not an apostle. He was one of the first deacons of the church.*)

Acts 8:4-8, 12-13

[4]Those who had been scattered preached the word wherever they went. [5]Philip went down to a city in Samaria and proclaimed the Christ there. [6]When the crowds heard Philip and saw the miraculous signs he did, they all paid close attention to what was said. [7]With shrieks, evil spirits came out of many, and many paralytics and cripples were healed. [8]So there was great joy in that city. . . [12]But when they believed Philip as he preached the good news of the kingdom of God and the name of Jesus Christ, they were baptized, both men and women. [13]Simon himself believed and was baptized. And he followed Philip everywhere, astonished by the great signs and miracles he saw." *(Philip, like Stephen was not an apostle, but was considered one of the first deacons, and was also an evangelist. There is reason to believe that it was expected that the New Testament evangelist would move in healing and miracles.)*

Acts 11:19-21

[19]Now those who had been scattered by the persecution in connection with Stephen traveled as far as Phoenicia, Cyprus and Antioch, telling the message only to Jews. [20]Some of them, however, men from Cyprus and Cyrene, went to Antioch and began to speak to Greeks also, telling them the good news about the Lord Jesus. [21]***The***

Lord's hand was with them, and a great number of people believed and turned to the Lord." *(The Lord's hand was a way of speaking of the power and presence of God and in Acts most likely indicated signs and wonders. These people were neither apostles or deacons. They were just believers.)*

B) In summary, many of our theological positions regarding healing have been developed based upon our experience rather than the clear meaning of the Bible.

C) For example, the anti-supernaturalism of Liberalism, would not be able to appeal to seminary students if they had experienced the supernatural in their Christian faith. The need to demythologize miracles such as the multiplication of bread – as Barclay does in his commentaries – would not appeal to someone who has experienced the multiplication of food. The need to demythologize the raising of the dead would not have an intellectual appeal to students who know persons who were raised from the dead in Jesus' name. Healing would not need to be demythologized when you have seen the deaf hear, the blind see, paraplegics walk, stroke victims restored, cancers disappear, and diabetics in last stages with neuropathy totally healed. In my opinion, what has happened is a new mythological world has been created by those influenced by the rationalism of a closed scientific worldview. The true world is not limited to the rationalistic understanding of an older scientism.

D) Over time, these theological positions have become accepted as the "proper interpretation" of Scripture. They prevent individuals from allowing the Scriptures to speak for themselves. When there is a testimony that someone has experienced a healing or miracle, they are then considered not of God based upon poor biblical interpretation, i.e. either cessationist interpretations, dispensational interpretations, or liberal interpretations.

E) The challenge of reinterpreting the Bible in ways to justify the views of other non-Christian groups, movements. i.e. New Age, Christian Science.

Notes

Notes